Travels Wi

La Vélod

Mike Banks

Other books by Mike Banks

More than the Bike – A Summer of Madness

The Bleating of Warped Sheep – Jumping in the Snow

First published in 2019

Cover by Mike Banks

All photographs by Fenella and Mike Banks

Edited by Fenella and James Banks

For Fenella and James

For every journey they may undertake

Contents

Introduction

French Onion Soup

Ingredients

70g of butter

700g of finely chopped onions (red or white)

2 cloves of garlic

1 teaspoon of plain flour

200ml of wine (red for red onions, dry white for white onions)

1.5 litres of vegetable stock

Season to taste

Preparation

Melt butter and add onions. Cook slowly for 30 min

Add flour and garlic and stir well

Add wine and simmer for 5 min

Add stock and seasoning. Simmer for 20 min

Transfer to blender and blend until smooth

Serve with sprinkled Parmesan cheese and warm crusty bread.

Best enjoyed following a pleasant cycle ride along quiet country lanes.

As a Zen proverb states:

Over a supper of soup and bread, when asking a group of his students why they ride their bikes, following various answers, the fifth student replied, 'I ride my bike to ride my bike'.

The teacher moved and sat at the feet of the fifth student, and said, 'I am your disciple.'

In Preparation

Unreal Reality (The Kinks)

Not a big snake as snakes go, but it still took me by surprise when it became entangled in my front wheel. It didn't seem to be injured, but as our eyes locked I'd bet good money it was rather startled to find itself interwoven between my spokes, and I reckon more than a little annoyed as well.

I must admit it's not an everyday occurrence for me to cycle over snakes so I suppose some form of explanation wouldn't go amiss…….

Since climbing from my bike in the north of Scotland after my 2014 Summer of Madness, in which I completed my first triathlon, my 16th Great North Run and a Lands End to John o'Groats cycle ride (LEJOG), I contemplated if I ever attempted another long solo cycle ride, I should do so with a French summer sun warming my back. After all, when trying to cycle somewhere in the region of 1000 miles, my calf's, thighs and particularly my backside, would without doubt be warmed to the point of a semi-simmer, so why not let old Sol's shine warm my other bones through too I thought.

But thinking about another long distance bike ride is one thing, doing it is something else. Although, it wasn't until Christmas 2016 that the concept of what I was considering came to sneak up on me as a possible reality. Despite that reality arriving adorned in Christmas wrapping, with 'Lots of Love from Fenella' printed neatly on the attached gift tag. It was a Garmin cycle GPS unit, complete with European mapping, the official French La Vélodyssée Route booklet and a Christmas Card, which instead of having, 'Have Yourself a Peaceful Time, Christmas is Here', written inside, may as well have had instead, 'Get Your Arse in Gear, Cycle Time is Coming, xxx!' Perfect.

I had done a little preparatory cycling though, in the form of a cycling holiday in Belgium and Holland during the previous summer with Fenella, which had seemed a perfect way to get my body back to the rigours of exercise following a longish break from the bike due to bouts of ill health.

I'd begun my descent into illness during the closing stages of my LEJOG, when I'd collapsed whilst cycling, and then ended-up wandering dazed and confused among the congregation of an outdoor wedding. Something I've regretted ever since. So too I imagine did the bride and groom. Although I'm sure it will have added a little spice to their confabs, when they finally got around to showing relations who'd missed out on the occasion their wedding video. I picture them game-fully trying to convince people that the old bloke in the sweat-starched orange cycling shirt, leaning on a bike and staring stupidly at the lens, was a planned addition to their nuptials, a sort of sporting twist on the appearance of a chimney sweep.

I sincerely hope the newlyweds and their guests took my appearance as just a perfunctory blip on an otherwise perfect day. Likewise, I too considered my collapse to be a momentary blip on what had been, up to that point, a history of rude health. Unfortunately, it turned out to be less blip and more of a comic balloon. The following autumn I had another collapse, this time after completing a pleasant cycle along part of the eastern leg of the Trans Pennine Trail, finishing under the cavernous canopy of the towering Humber Bridge. But on that occasion, before I could meet Fenella, a lady who saw me fall called the emergency services, allowing me the thrilling opportunity of being stretchered into the rear-end of an ambulance to be whisked away towards the unfathomable logistical workings of the NHS, namely, Hull Royal Infirmary. Once there, I was hard-wired to various machines, one of which instructed the nursing staff I'd died. Which was rather surprising, as it was me who had to alert the staff to the alarm, and rather wasteful, as at the time I was merrily tucking into a cheese and pickle sandwich.

Of course, I survived, in fact it wasn't a bad sandwich at all, and I put no blame on it of what was to follow. Over the next few months I had more collapses, I lost my balance to the extent that at times I couldn't fathom what was up, down, or what was right or left. I began to tremble wildly from my right shoulder to the tips of my fingers, I had high blood pressure, low blood pressure, sometimes I suspected one half of me had alternating blood pressure whilst my other half had no blood at all,

9

and I felt nauseous for months on end. I dreaded the thought, but I began to seriously speculate I'd become pregnant.

All the while I traipsed around the Yorkshire hospitals, being poked, prodded, asked to stand on one leg and then walk along a white line, and once, injected with some extraordinary compound which bizarrely turned me radioactive for 24hrs and made me feel so exhausted it felt as if I'd cycled up and down the Three Peaks a few dozen times. It all proved to be of no avail. I'd become a medical mystery. Finally, I was given some medication to settle my blood pressure, advised to have a glass of red wine each evening (I kid you not) and given a two page pamphlet which looked like it had been produced in a kindergarten class by the kid who can't draw for toffee, showing stick men, doing dramatic exercises such as, 'sit on a chair and move your head first to the left, and then to the right.' After months of testing I was given no diagnosis of what was causing me to collapse, my constant dizziness, my right-sided shakes and my swinging blood pressure. It's so comforting to know that I've paid my National Insurance for forty odd years.

So as we headed for the port of Hull to catch the overnight ferry to Zeebrugge it was with an air of medical trepidation on my part and an air of worry on Fenella's part as to whether I was going to be OK during our venture.

Thankfully I was, and having cycled around 350 miles, physically and mentally the holiday was just what I needed to help me re-connect with the bike, although not particularly with the bike I used during our trip, a heavy, rather uncomfortable mountain bike I bought on-line for £50 from a Royal Engineer in Sheffield who was being redeployed to Kenya. But, on our return, I knew I'd re-found my cycling legs, plus my self-assurance in the fact that I could cope with a good few miles of day in, day out cycle tripping. I'd set myself up nicely for an autumn and winter of training. However, when I use the term 'training', please don't misunderstand me in the sense to imagine me spending hours down at the gym burning the pounds in punishing spinning classes, pummelling mile upon painful mile on dizzy inducing treadmills, or lathered in sweat yanking bits of metal around. No, I mean during the months between October 2016 and the summer of 2017, to increase stamina I walked to the fish shop instead of driving, to build strength I wore a windup watch instead of a battery operated model, and I had a few pleasant bike rides when and where I fancied. Nevertheless, I placed myself on a strict diet designed to enhance my natural athletic prowess. I swapped red wine for white, fried chips for oven, and with the knowledge that certain fatty dairy products can cause soaring cholesterol, I swapped cheese flavoured crisps for plain. It was arduous but the benefits were staggering. I saved at least £10 on petrol, stamina wise I could walk up two flights of stairs with only one brief 3 minute respite and my overall strength developed to the point where I began to order three chilli meals from the local Indian take-away, rather than my previous pathetic two. Oh, and I got to see some great bits of South Yorkshire and North Lincolnshire.

The area in which I live has the National Cycle Network Route (NCN) 62 bordering my doorstep. This forms part of the Trans Pennine Route, running from Hornsea on the East Coast to Southsea on the West. It also has numerous branch routes running north and south. Up until March 2017, I still hadn't fully decided on my final course, although I was certain it would include La Vélodyssée, which is an 80% off-road route along the west coast of France, and although it seemed to be pretty flat when viewed on paper I knew, as most coastal routes do, it would provide me with numerous short sharp climbs. To get me used to a touch of climbing, part of my training included a few trips across the Pennines from Doncaster to Chester. But my weekly training ride throughout the autumn and winter months was along a branch of NCN 62, the NCN 65, from home to York. York is a handy place for me to cycle to, the route has numerous café stops along the way and in the city itself. York also boasts to having one of the better cycle shops in the UK, Cycle Heaven, a great place for cyclists and non-cyclists to investigate. Developed within a disused factory, the shop has almost everything a discerning cyclist could ever need, including my book, More Than The Bike (A Summer of Madness), and Café 68, which offers some of the most scrumptious, home-baked cakes in Yorkshire.

It was along this route that I began to test out the possibilities of my new Christmas gift GPS unit, although

I had difficulties attaching it to my bike's handlebars, and I realised the handlebar base-unit must be from a different model. Informing the staff at Cycle Heaven about the problem they were extremely apologetic and without any fuss or dramatics immediately provided me with a replacement. When I arrived home to tell Fenella about the shops marvellous service, she gave me that same withering stare I often get from friends and family, sighed, and said, 'I didn't buy it from Cycle Heaven, I bought it from Cycle Supreme in Doncaster'.

As winter loosened its grip on the countryside and BBC Springwatch once again filled the TV schedules with its daily dirge of over enthusiastic grinning, giggling and gurning presenters. I made the final decisions about my route. I planned to cycle from the beginning of La Vélodyssée in North Devon, along the Devon Coast to Coast Route, (NCN 27), ferry from Plymouth to Roscoff, and then down the West Coast of France to San Sebastián in Northern Spain. I would begin at a northern point, cycle southwards for around a 1000 miles, and finish at a northern point, my own twist on the famous French road race 'The Hell of the North'.

Having experience of a 1000 mile plus cycle trip, when completing LEJOG and having wildly overestimated my stamina capabilities, thinking I could complete the journey in 14 days, but taking 24 days, using a combination of camping, B&B and hotels, I allowed myself the whole of July 2017 to complete this trip. Hopefully, this would reduce the chances of my illnesses' reoccurring, and give Fenella and myself the possibility of enjoying the jaunt, rather than it becoming a nightmarish slog against the clock. However, I managed to come down with a touch of Bronchitis about a month before my planned start, but thankfully a visit to the doc's, a course of penicillin and a little rest soon saw me right. It was during this period that I contacted my favoured charity Yorkshire Cancer Research (YCR) and agreed to use the trip as a means of raising funds for the fantastic work they do in their aim of one day beating this scourge of a disease. In turn I was also contacted by a reporter from the local rag, Doncaster Free Press, who wrote a glowing article about my plans and kindly helped to promote my charity to the Yorkshire reading public. Continuing this theme I agreed that half the proceeds from my book, More Than The Bike, would be donated to YCR.

In mid-April, I'm sure just to help divert my thoughts away from my trip, Teresa May kindly decided to have a general Election, and so during early May, the other May, the one you can put your trust in as always remaining strong and stable in its calendar position, as the politicians headed to Yorkshire for an Election Question Time special, as a change from cycling I took myself off for a hike around 17 miles of the Doncaster Way. Just as I finished my ramble, I nearly ended-up under the wheels of a car. As I walked rather painfully along the pavement, a driver pulled out of a supermarket car park and ran straight into me. Luckily she was only travelling very slowly, but nevertheless I still ended-up on her car bonnet. I've seen many a movie where the hero clings manfully onto a speeding '66 Chrysler Imperial, or a '75 Ford Gran Torin, under a New York underpass, or on Golden Gate Bridge, shouting threats at a car-load of snarling gangsters. But it just didn't seem to be like that for me as I perched precariously on the front end of a Vauxhall Corsa in a Sainsbury's car park exit. To make me feel even more insubstantial the driver didn't even realise I was there until her daughter shouted, 'Mam, watch it, there's an old bloke on the car bonnet, with a beard!' At this point the driver suddenly stopped allowing me to slide ungracefully back onto terra-firma. To be honest I believe the only reason why she stopped so quickly wasn't for any concerns about my safety, rather I got the impression she was filled with dread in case Jeremy Corbyn had leapt on to her car in a last minute bid for her vote. From that point onwards I decided for the remainder of my training I'd be voting to stick to cycling, I'm sure it was going to be far safer than walking the pavements of Doncaster!

Thanks to Fenella, a bonus I had over my LEJOG trip was I didn't have to plan my own route, it was all prearranged for me in my La Vélodyssée Route Guide, besides if I did wander off-track I had my GPS unit as backup, what could possibly go wrong?

So as glorious June swept in, and the ferry to France booked for the 3 July, my preparations for a cycling and camping adventure were just about complete, albeit a couple of articles I thought might come in handy; namely a tent and a bike!

15

I'd sold the tent we used during LEJOG at the completion of that trip, because due to my dabbles with illness it seemed unlikely that in a few years' time I'd be planning something similar. As for a bike, I had a few models tucked away in the garage, a small wheeled folder with a limited choice of gearing, designed to be more commuter than long distance tourer. A 1970's 'road classic', which in reality was a rusting old crock with wobbly wheels, and my pre-mentioned heavy mountain bike. None realistically being suitable for such a long excursion. Also, unused since my LEJOG, my trusty old mate 'Rocky.' But it was with a heavy heart that I had to admit, although during LEJOG Rocky had been a rock of a bike, never letting me down once, by the end of my trip I'd come to painfully realise he was actually way too small for me. So in effect, for a cycling and camping adventure we were both 'tentless and bikeless', not a great state to be in with departure so close at hand.

Fenella set about finding a tent for us, and seemingly with what I can only assume to be female, or to my mind more likely, mystic abilities, she soon had one ordered and despatched, leaving me, with only male proficiencies at hand, to find a bike.

I remember about 15 years ago when trying to buy a touring bike, I'd trailed fruitlessly around cycle shops searching in vain, the only choice being mountain bike after mountain bike, with the odd touring bike sneaking in the selection, usually being disguised as a mountain bike. This time around my search was annoyingly similar. Following the extraordinary success of British

16

road and track cyclists in the last trio of Olympics, and the Sky Team clinging on to the Tour de France Maillot Jaune as their own property, most bike shops were brimming with expensive replica road bikes, and although a vast range of mountain bikes could be found, medium priced touring cycles still remained awfully thin on the ground. It is true that if you wander into a well-stocked cycle retailer, with fifteen hundred to a couple of thousand quid ready to leap from your pocket, they'll soon sort you out with a bike that looks as if it could take on a world tour no problem. But I'd discovered finding an appropriate bike which wasn't the price of a decent second-hand car had become a tricky challenge. In the end I set my sights on a German engineered Cube cycle as the best achievable option. I investigated the possibility of ordering one on-line, but I was wary on three accounts. I'd be buying a bike I hadn't even seen 'in the flesh', let alone had a test-ride on, and with our departure looming, I couldn't be sure of receiving one in time, enquiries demonstrated that most internet retailers didn't keep bikes in stock, but ordered them from global warehouses. Also, it was difficult to ensure that the version glowingly described in the ads would be the one I'd receive, as some on-line retailers were off-loading lower-spec 2015 and 2016 bikes instead of 2017 models.

Then I discovered the Cube Store, JC Cook, at 'Sunny Scunny', arguably the best cycle shop north of the English Channel.

I'd come across the shop by chance buying inner-tubes for my mountain bike, the cycle I'd resigned myself as having to use, like it or lump it. I'd wandered into the store on a sultry June evening, my being vibrating with the possibility of finding 'the one'. I thought I'd entered Nirvana. Surrounded by shimmering svelte road cycles and chiselled mountain bikes, a vision of perfection suddenly magnetised me to the core, a Cube Touring Pro. Magnificent in gun-metal grey, with enticing swirls of lime green, a splendour of sophisticated stylishness. I gripped it's handlebars with a measured firmness, I lightly ran my hand along its flowing top-tube and caressed the smooth suppleness of its sculptured saddle. Slipping my sunglasses off to feast my eyes further, I delicately palmed its price tag. Bloody hell! I couldn't afford that, it was at least £1000 more than I'd expected. Distraught, I turned away to face the evening; miserable, forsaken.....alone.

I was in the store region a fortnight later with Fenella, collecting household items for our son James, who was in the process of buying his first property. 'Why not call in and see if they've had any other bikes delivered since you were last here', reasoned Fenella.
'Na, it'll be a waste of time', I countered, 'there'll be nothing worth seeing'. But in the end I gave in to reason, and with a manner bordering on solemnity I wandered back into the shop. I could see at once the same selection of bikes were on display, including the Touring Pro. Pointing it out to Fenella I told her that was

the cycle I really liked, but at £1600 it was far too expensive.

She wandered over to have a neb. She too looked at the price tag. 'I thought you said it was £1600', she queried.
'It is, and I'm not paying that much for a bike', I replied.
'No it isn't', she told me, 'its £600. Did you have your glasses on when you read the price?'
'Well, erm, I'm not sure,' I mumbled, 'erm, I think I could've had my sun specs instead'.
'Oh lord above, give me strength', came her exasperated reply.

As we were talking, Tony from Cube sauntered our way and asked if we needed any help. I find whenever a sales person asks if 'you need any help', that sales line can usually be translated into, 'don't buy that, buy this, it's not any better but it costs nearly twice as much and I need the commission', but I didn't get that impression with Tony. I believed he really wanted to help whether I bought anything or not. We got chatting and I told him of my plans, my need for a bike and my attraction to the Touring Pro. 'Well it's a great bike, it's built for what you need, but you really need to know if it's right for you, take it out and give it a spin if you want, you might find you like it, or find you might not, it's no problem, it's a personal thing with bikes', advised Tony. Sound advice I thought, so out for a spin I went. I knew within two pedal revolutions it was the bike coming to France with me, it just felt...'right'.

Back in the shop having agreed on a deal, Tony asked me what sort of pedals I wanted on the bike? This confused me somewhat, looking down it seemed to have a perfectly good pair of pedals already attached. When I mentioned this to Tony he furthered, 'what I mean is, which pedals do you want me to put on your bike to match your cycling shoes?'

I was even more confused, cycling shoes? 'I usually cycle in these', I answered pointing to my scruffy pair of well-used converse, 'I've had them ages, they're nice and comfy, do I need different pedals for them?'

'Them!' came his indignantly surprised reply. 'You can't cycle all those miles in them, you'll hardly be able to put your feet on the ground after a few days. You need shoes with properly hardened soles, and I'd advise you to use clips and a pair of SDP pedals, then you'll find you're using the right cycling muscles all the way along your legs right up to your hips. I'll fit pedals which have shoe clips on one side and are ordinary platform pedals on the reverse side, then you can have the benefit of both types of pedal in one model'.

'Blimey!' I reacted, 'to do this ride I reckoned maybe I'd need a hard soul, but I never thought I'd need all three of 'em'.

I began to think there was more to buying a bike than I thought. I was right. An hour or so later I'd left the store with a new bike on order; new pedals, new cycling shoes, new SDP clips, plus a slack handful of scientifically based energy bars and alcohol infused jelly cubes, and an extremely large pack of chocolate and mint flavoured

Torq Recovery mix, which Tony promised me was almost magical in its ability to refuel a depleted body.

To be fair, Tony didn't charge me for the SDP pedals, the shoe clips, or the energy jellies. But, I spent the remainder of the day in a bemused fug of how in the past I'd managed to cycle thousands of miles, on second-hand bikes, using plastic pedals, wearing worn-out clipless converse pumps, and having only a cup of tea and a KitKat as a means of recovery.

My bike was delivered the Tuesday before the weekend of our departure. It would have been so good to have had a stress-free few days trying my bike out, making those small, but vital adjustments to sizing and riding position, trying for a fit on the cycle carrier and titivating final details to our overall plans. There was to be no chance. The previous Friday Fenella had retired from 20 years of teaching, and as well as the bewildering shock of forthcoming freedom, she was expected at a number of leaving do's. I was working my last week of the academic year, trying to complete all the last minute paperwork that dogs the life of anyone daft enough to work in education, and after waiting week upon week to receive the keys to his first house, James got the call at 5pm on the Thursday of that week.

My bike was shoved in a corner of the conservatory and I never even had a chance to glance at it until I wheeled it out for attachment to the car cycle carrier, so much for those personalised adjustments. Fenella became exhausted with a confusing mixture of relief, excitement and sadness and James didn't quite know what to do first. The result was, after spending Thursday evening, Friday and early Saturday morning helping James move into his house, by Saturday lunchtime, instead of making sure all the items we needed for the trip had been packed in the car with care, most things were just lobbed in willy-nilly fashion, and when I tried to attach my bike onto the carrier I discovered to my dismay it wouldn't fit without scraping all of its paintwork from its frame. The only option was to buy a different style of carrier. Telephoning around we managed to locate a towball mounted carrier from a well-known motor accessories retailer, but they didn't have one already assembled. By the time Fenella had collected it from Doncaster, while I'd childishly stormed around the garden having a major paddy of frustration, and then I'd ineffectually and foul temperedly manipulated a selection of tools to assemble the damn thing, the afternoon had passed and evening was rolling in. Befuddled, we finally set-off for the 300 mile trip to Devon at 5pm, not ideal given that apart from a rushed breakfast, we hadn't eaten all day, and I had to begin cycling across the county the following Sunday morning to ensure we caught the ferry to France on Monday evening.

Without as so much as a toilet break along the way, we arrived at our digs in Braunton at about 10pm, and following a rushed book-in and a quick hello to our hosts, we hit the town on the hunt for nosh. Luckily we managed to catch Squire's Fish Restaurant before it slammed its doors for the night. Although, the only food on offer was a selection of deep-fried bits-and-bobs that the earlier customers had apparently rejected in favour of a balanced meal. Still, despite the insinuation that it's the early birds who acquire the juicy morsels, being the opposites, at that late hour, as we balanced on a nearby wall munching away, we were thankful for any type of hot grub, be it balanced or not.

We knew before we called it a night we should say thanks to our hosts for waiting for us to arrive. Being a private run guesthouse as opposed to a commercial hotel they wouldn't normally have remained open so late, but having kindly given us an entrance key on arrival, by the time we'd got back, they'd scarpered off to beddie-byes. We promised ourselves we would catch-up with them in the morning. Fenella also headed for slumber, leaving me to have a reflective spell to myself. Sat in the guest lounge, knowing my adventure would begin in earnest first thing the following morning, the certainty of the situation finally came to smack me in the face. Up until that point in time, despite the actualities of my research, our cycling holiday and even the purchase of my bike, I'd somehow never fully grasped the veracity of my intentions. Sat alone, with just the rhythmic ticking of the mantelpiece carriage-clock for company, I gazed glassy-eyed into the Devon darkness and realised the enormity of what I'd set myself up to do. Unreal reality was about to warp into actuality.

La Vélodyssée

Part 1

Doing Devon - Train in Vain (The Clash)

I awoke surprisingly refreshed and ready for the day. Perhaps it was eager anticipation that this was the beginning of what was going to be a wonderful adventure that had me leaping from the bed and almost through the bedroom door, or more likely it was the inviting waft of a breakfast fry-up. Whichever, Fenella's stern warning that the other breakfasters may prefer to eat without seeing me clad only in an, 'Education is Important, But Bikes are More Importanter' T-shirt and tartan boxers which halted my headlong rush for food. I'd quite forgotten that other guests would be staying there too.

Appropriately attired and ordering breakfast we got a chance to thank Julie our host for her kindness the night before. Constructed in 1798, The Brookfield, Braunton is a superb Georgian built guesthouse that couldn't be a more ideal location for cyclists, as it stands virtually next to the Tarka Trail Cycle Way, which forms part of the NCR 27 the Devon Coast to Coast route. More like a 5 star boutique hotel than your average B&B, it's also an ideal place for walkers, golfers, surfers and for folk who just want to chill out for a few days. As we battled our way through the huge full English breakfasts beautifully cooked by Julie and her staff, eves-dropping on the other guest's conversations, it appeared I wasn't the only person focused on a sporting day ahead. A table of four had hiking maps spread across their table and were working out the miles they intended to cover that day, and from the exchanges between a couple of chaps sat adjacent from us, who were earnestly discussing their preferences for googlies, leg-slips and groin protection, they were either off cricketing, or were planning some other sporting activity that didn't fully spring to mind.

Then it was my turn. Not to let my leg slip anywhere untoward, but time to slip into my cycling gear, slip into cycling mode, and slip into my La Vélodyssée. The first part was easy, and it felt good to be back in cycling clothes once again. Although I took care when pulling on my cycle shorts to double check I had them the right way round. Having once experienced the unique and rather compressing sensation of wearing tight gel-padded shorts back-to-front on a ride to Scunthorpe, it was not a feeling I wished to revisit. With the bike unloaded from the car, I posed for a couple of photos under the hanging basket outside The Brookfield, which from the position Fenella had me stand made it look as if I was trying to balance a miniature garden on my head. Then, with nothing but sporting glory laying ahead of me, I threw caution to the wind, threw my leg across the saddle, locked my shoes into my SDP pedals and threw my bike forwards towards Spain. Then I fell off. Well, to be more precise I wobbled 20 yards sideways into the confines of a large privet hedge.

Not a brilliant start, given that I hadn't even managed to get myself out of the guesthouse car park. I'd been so intent about concentrating on my feet being fastened in my pedals I'd lost focus on all else, including balance. I was riding like a child who'd just had their stabilisers removed for the first time. Propped-up in the hedge, freeing my feet from the pedals, I realised I was going to need much more practice with my SDP's than I'd first imagined, and a tightly packed car park was not the ideal place in which to begin.

Feet free and with a tad more dignity, I made my way to the start of the off-road Tarka Trail cycleway. This is a route I know well having cycled it numerous times while holidaying in and around North Devon. Hugging the shoreline of the River Taw estuary between Braunton and Barnstable, the route passes by the Royal Marines Base, Chivenor. Now primarily home to Commando Logistic Regiment, Royal Marines, RMB Chivenor has around 1200 personnel on site from all three services, including 24 Commando Regiment, Royal Engineers and 22 Squadron, 'A' Flight Search and Rescue Force, RAF. If you're ever unlucky enough to need rescuing from the seas off the North Devon coastline it will be into one of the bright yellow helicopters flying from RMB Chivenor you will find yourself being winched. But as I passed by all seemed quiet and peaceful, although no doubt the helicopter crews were still on standby just in case the call came through.

It was still early, yet a good few fellow cyclists, dedicated joggers and sauntering strollers were out and about

26

enjoying the warming air and watching the wading curlews, greenshanks and dunlins grubbing for morsels in the glistening silt left in the low tide estuary. All the while I was trying to find my feet with my new bike. I recognised almost instantly it was a terrific machine, running slickly across the hard cycleway surface, I ran up and down the gearing, tested the ultra-smooth modulation of the disc brakes and persisted with locking my shoes in the pedals and attempting to release them without the need of any nearby hedgerows, but I just couldn't get the action effortless or efficient. I began to think back to how my mate Graham Jarvis, who always uses lock pedals, told me about how he learnt to unlock his feet. He confided that he mentally chanted the Brotherhood of Man ditty, 'Save All Your Kisses for Me', while at the same time doing the little shimmy accompaniment, which is a sort of feet twisting and elbow flapping movement, which bizarrely, he said always allowed him to release his feet easily. Was I that desperate to begin singing Brotherhood of Man songs? It turned out I was, and it turned out it worked for me too. The dilemma was I began to run through the Brotherhood's back repertoire. Just what the other Tarka Trail users thought of me merrily whizzing along, singing such 'classics' as Figaro, Angelo and United We Stand, even today, doesn't bare thinking about!

Crossing the River Taw, via the Western Bypass Bridge in Barnstaple which opened in 2007 to ease traffic away from the town's grade 1 listed building, Long Bridge, which dates back to the late-13th century, I made my way along the opposite bank towards Bideford. Along this section of the Tarka Trail I was cycling a disused railway line which originally had linked Barnstaple and Bideford. Intended to be part of the Taw-Torridge Country Park, the line was sold off by British Rail in 1987 for the princely sum of £515,000. As I and the other trail cyclists enjoyed that fine Sunday morning I reflected that British Rail's loss was the cyclists gain.

But the trail has witnessed trains running again in more recent years, although they were a great deal smaller and less passenger and goods accommodating than those originally puffing along the line; toy trains, under the enthusiastic control of James May, as part of his Toy Stories TV series. May's first toy train was ran as a Guinness World Record attempt in 2009, when he tried to run a model train borrowed from the Hornby company along a ten mile stretch from Barnstaple to Bideford. Unfortunately, despite overcoming an incident of vandalism, when two pence coins were dropped across the track reducing the power output, the train 'gave up the ghost' due to a mechanical fault at Instow, some 3 miles short of the intended destination.

Not one to give in to bad fortune, May had another crack at being a Tarka Trail train controller in 2011, this time using his own 1972 Flying Scotsman Hornby original, in a head to head race against a team of German enthusiasts in what became known as, 'The Great Train Race'. With each team running three trains, and the Germans setting off from Bideford, while May and his team mate, the wine expert Oz Clarke, set off from Barnstable, for the enthusiastic crowd of bystanders it must have seemed like 1966 all over again, albeit minus any sporting prowess. But bad fortune struck May a second time. After an early battery misfortune for the Germans, they settled into the contest with stoic efficiency and were so confident of winning they had time to calmly stop for ice cream refreshments at Fremington Quay. No such comfort for May, as he became hot under the collar by being forced to stop to make running repairs to his beloved train at Yelland, leaving the Germans to claim victory. So, for May and Clarke it proved to be a train in vain and not quite 1966 after all.

I fancied stopping at Fremington too, and while it was a bit early for ice cream, a coffee would have gone down well. But seeing no signs of Fenella I carried on to Instow. I still felt very much on home turf cycle-wise, and as I approached the town I remembered a couple of years ago when I had a head-to-head race into town with another trail user, which I'm happy to report I'd won hands down. Although rather ashamedly I'd also better admit that my victory wasn't down to any sporting prowess on my part and was more likely down to my competitor's electric wheelchair running out of battery power.

Finding no one to race with on that particular Sunday morning, waiting for Fenella to arrive, I contented myself by sitting on the quayside wall sipping from my bidon and looking across the River Torridge towards Appledore, the village on the opposite shoreline, where

29

some kind of event was in progress. I couldn't accurately make out what was happening as all I could hear was the muddled reverberating babble of several competing PA system announcers. I later discovered it was the World Championship Crabbing Contest in full swing, in which Team Ayres scooped the first prize with a catch of 164 crabs. Crabtivating!

I waited around for 15 minutes or so, but I knew I'd have to move on. I felt confident that Fenella and I would catch-up with each other at some point during the morning. It appeared that the direct routing of the cycle track, as opposed to the winding Devon roads Fenella had to drive, had allowed me to get ahead of her.

I was still ahead as I made my way through historic Bideford, a town which grew from a location where it was possible to cross, or 'ford', the River Torridge. The etymology of the town's name means "by the ford". Luckily, today's Torridge crosses' don't have to get their feet quiet so damp as the wooden 'Long Bridge', (the Devon folk sure like that name for their bridges), was built in 1286, later to be replaced by the masonry arched bridge which still spans the river.

For those who like to puff a cigarette, or like me, those who detest the things, Bideford has a rich history. It was into the town's port, where on July 27th 1586, Sir Walter Raleigh first landed tobacco following his voyage from Virginia. Although, despite history giving the credit to Raleigh, it is more likely that the horrid stuff had actually made it into the country in 1565. Bizarrely, the other import Raleigh introduced, potatoes, were believed to be dangerous to health, while tobacco was expounded as being good for one's constitution, even medically helping those with breathing problems. As I cycled through the port I didn't spy too many smokers, or for that matter any signs warning about potato infection, maybe the area had recently been swabbed by a team of highly accomplished cleaning technicians.

Between Bideford and Great Torrington I began to muse about a name for my bike. I view bikes as presence's who have individual personalities, found in shape, colour, feel, profile, weight, balance, gearing and the distinct manner in which they traverse roads and tracks, I find them all wonderfully idiosyncratic characters, entities of living art. It's a concept in which I and Fenella just don't agree on. To Fenella, a cycle is simply a machine, albeit she finds some machines to be more appealing than others, but fundamentally she views them just as objects on which to ride from place to place. So choosing a name for my bike was important to me. Staying with the art theme and considering the manufactures name, that most of the frame tubing was cuboid and my ultimate destination was Spain, I settled on the name Pablo. After all, I reckoned good 'ole Picasso must have had a soft spot for cubes too.

As I pulled into the station at Great Torrington, taking the town's name to heart, I made a great, and what could have been a disastrous mistake, something which could have ended my trip right there and then. Having sang The Brotherhood for most of the way along the trail, as I came to a stop on the platform, I suddenly went into Bucks Fizz mode and started singing, 'Making Your Mind Up', different song, different dance routine, a routine which didn't help me unlock my shoes. There I precariously balanced, steel fencing on one side, a five foot drop onto the rusting railway lines on the other, while I furiously tried to release my feet. But no matter how I twisted, wiggled and yanked I couldn't release my shoes, and bit by bit I realised I was going to tumble onto the rails below. But just as my momentum inched towards the tipping point, mercifully my left foot shot free, and I slammed it to the ground as an anchor of deliverance. If I'd gone over the best I could have escaped with was buckled wheels, a dented frame, bent forks and only one or two broken bones. I immediately recognised 3 things;   1) I'd had a lucky escape, 2) no matter the benefits of a correct pedal-to-foot posture, I couldn't safely trust the SPD side of my pedals until I'd made some adjustment to their locking tensions, and 3) no more dangerously misleading middle-of-the-road 80's ditties during this trip.

Meeting Fenella I calmed myself down and regained a little composure with a large mug of coffee and a scone just slightly smaller than my cycling helmet, bought from the Puffing Billy Restaurant located in what once was the Station Masters house.

Originally built by the North Devon Railway in 1872, Great Torrington Station was operated by London and South Western Railway. It became famous as the starting point for the daily 'Milk Run', in which two express trains delivered milk from the Devonshire dairies to London, through Waterloo and Clapham Junction stations, a service which continued up until 1978. It's unclear how Londoners manage to get their daily ration from that date onwards, but whenever I'm visiting the place it may explain why so many folk order such bizarre drinks as; The Bulletproof, coffee laced with peanut butter and olive oil, The Vincent Vega, named after John Travolta's character in Pulp Fiction and is made from Coca-Cola, vanilla syrup and a shot of black expresso, and Elephant Poop Coffee, in which the coffee beans are ground after first passing through an elephants digestive system. But as a northerner, and perhaps rather boringly, I took my coffee with just a small slop of milk and without the need for any oil, a fading disco dancer, or the arse end of an elephant.

After Great Torrington the off-road section of the Tarka Trail continued for about 10 miles, suddenly ending to join the A386 on the outskirts of Meeth. I then had an uncomfortable climb into the market town of Hatherleigh. The smallest town in North Devon, Hatherleigh still boasts a live cattle market every Monday, followed by a live poultry market every Tuesday. But on that particular Sunday there was little sign of any kind of life apart from a few kids lazily looping around in circles on their push scooters outside the local Co-op. Freewheeling through town, still on the A386, I tried in vain to pick-up the signs for the NCR 27, but it was no use, I couldn't find one anywhere. The difficulty was that at 4.30pm, the heat of the day was at its highest, the road was twisting, hilly and chock-a-block with exhausted Sunday drivers, all speeding back from the coastal resorts with cars loaded with overheated argumentative kids, dozing grandparents and farting dogs. I know this because as least two nearly hit me, and from the interior of both came the intermingled racket of screeching 10 year olds, snoring elders, and from the opened back windows, the heady aroma of canine venting. It was not a pleasant, or safe road for a cyclist to be on. Giving up on finding the NCR 27, I knew if I could find the B3216 to Jacobstowe I would be able to use a series of quiet lanes leading to Okehampton, where I planned to stop for the day. But finding that road appeared to be just as difficult. Following another close call with a speeding driver, I pulled into the grass verge just past Basset's Cross for a slurp from my bidon, and looking back I spotted the road sign for Jacobstowe. It was actually situated about twenty yards into the B3216 itself, making it almost impossible to spot from the main road. If I hadn't looked back I would never have seen it. Maybe the local's didn't want to be disturbed by anyone who didn't know their way around without the use of road signs and had hidden it away from prying eyes, but it hadn't worked on me, ha! About half a mile along the B3216 I saw a sign for the NCR 27, where all the others had been since leaving Hatherleigh was anybody's guess. It seemed that this part of Devon had their own customs where road directions and signage were concerned. But it was reassuring to know I was at last back on the right track.

I met Fenella in the centre of Okehampton and loaded Pablo on the car, as our hotel for the night was a few miles out of town in the village of Sourton. I say hotel, but knowing we planned to camp for most nights once we were in France, we were poshing-it-up in a converted 15thC manor house, the Collaven Manor Hotel.

Originally owned by the Hamilton family and reputedly associated with Lady Hamilton, Collaven Manor was a fantastic and luxurious place to stay after my first day in the saddle. We then settled ourselves in the small snug, where Fenella had a well-deserved martini and I had a tipple of my favourite local brew, Jail Ale.

After our disorganised rush down to Devon the previous day, followed by 47 miles on the bike for me, and about 70 miles of driving along narrow twisting Devonshire roads for Fenella, neither of us fancied moving far for the evening, and despite only serving what Jeff our host termed as, 'light meals', we decided to eat in the hotel. We were not disappointed. Jeff's beetroot salad turned out to be a gigantic platter of cheeses, hams, salads, fruits, olives, pickles and garnishes all served with a large basket of wonderfully crusty bread, freshly baked that afternoon by his wife Jacqui. It was absolutely scrumptious.

Situated in such an impressive setting, it seemed a shame not to have a gander at the surroundings of the hotel. So partly to ease our digestions and partly just to be nosey, we had a wander around the gardens, accompanied by a quartet of Jeff's and Jacqui's cats, who curiously all shared the same initial name consonant as their owners, accordingly along came James, Jango, Jill and Jasmine. The evening was beginning to draw in, the heavy sky to threaten with rain, and a humid mist hung low above the dampening lawns. Just the right environment for the local mossies' to enjoy and cunningly plan their devilish raids on human flesh, and resourcefully raid they certainly did. Not on me, but unfortunately for Fenella, on her shoulders and upper arms. Although, as is usually the case, the results of their attacks was not going to be evident until the following morning.

Before retiring for the night I had my first 'dose' of Torq, the recovery drink which Tony at the Cube Store had been so enthusiastic about. Mixing the chocolate coloured powder in 600ml of cold water, slightly gagging at its smell and with initial doubt, I gulped it down as fast as I could. I guessed the worth of the stuff would be found over the following days. Laying snug in our four poster, listening to the light patter of rain hitting the windows, a precipitation which had begun following our evening stroll, I considered the fact that Fenella and I could well have been kipping down for the night in the same room that Horatio and his muse Emma, had spent many a night planning their own Velodyssee, although in their case it being a voyage of furtive passion rather than one of two wheeled adventure.

It was still smattering with rain when we awoke, not what the doctor had ordered so early in the trip, neither was the state of Fenella's upper arms where the mosquitoes had bitten. At least a couple of her bites had blistered and instead of being annoyingly itchy were instead uncomfortably painful to her touch. This had happened the previous summer when holidaying in Devon and had resulted in her needing medical assistance. Fortunately, if any fortune could be taken from the situation, the medication required could be bought over the counter at a chemist. But on the unfortunate side of things, there wasn't a chemist in Sourton village, with the nearest chemist likely to stock the medication being in Tavistock. Therefore, over breakfast we made adjustments to my day's route and planned a course which would take me through the town centre.

Thankfully, Fenella's bites did little to kill her appetite and like me she ordered the full works, with both of us knowing this could be our last chance of eating a full English for a good few weeks. While we were dining, Mazey, another guest joined us in the dining room. She had arrived late the previous evening and was breaking her journey from Oxford down to Penzance in Cornwall. However, as we got chatting and she discovered we were heading for France, she haughtily informed us that, 'she absolutely hated France and the French'. It turned out this was based on her having once ordered an espresso laced with chocolate from what she termed as, 'nothing more than a scruffy Parisian street café', only to be told that they would, 'do no such thing to good coffee', along with a recommendation that she visited the local McDonalds if she required such a concoction. Ha, ha. Good for them I thought. I've heard many folk call the French for being 'standoffish and aloof', but when faced with such English snobbery who can blame them? We love France, and while every place has the odd bodd or three, we've found that if we're prepared to have a go at speaking French, no matter how bad our vernacular, and believe me, my Yorkshire accented French is appalling, the French are friendly hospitable folk, who will help you in any way they can. We wouldn't have been heading there if this wasn't the case.

By the time we'd finished breakfast and I'd retrieved Pablo from the disused carriage house in which Jeff had kindly let me store him for the night, the rain had turned into a heavy curtain of drizzle, the kind that saturates all it touches. I reluctantly decided to dress in my rain gear until the weather cleared. Leaving Fenella to have a more leisurely departure, turning right at the gates of Collaven Manor onto the A386 I had a short hop to Bearslake Inn, where I once again joined an off-road section of the NCR 27.

I knew the next couple of hours would find me riding the mid-Devon hill country, and as soon as I started along the trail this was the case, although to begin with the uphill gradient of the track was fairly gentle. My difficulty was, despite the inclement weather, I was boiling-up inside my waterproof jacket. After about 15 minutes I became so uncomfortable I stripped back down to my short-sleeved shirt, deciding I'd be happier being soaked by the rain as opposed to being saturated in my own sweat. A couple of miles later I caught-up with another rider, and matching his pace we rode together for the next few miles until the track re-joined the A386 adjacent to Linford Gorge . This was Callan, a Scotsman, originally from Gargunnock, east of Stirling, who had taken up residency in the Okehampton area, out for his daily ride along the track. Having heard the Scots have more words to describe rain than the Eskimos have for snow, I expected Callan to give me a fantastic descriptive variant on our rather damp conditions, with descriptors such as; yasking, drookit, or hooring it in fudders. He didn't disappoint, turning to me and peering through the sheeting rain, he declared, 'fuckin' shitty weather, I fuckin' hate it when it's pissing it down like this!' Although when it came to local cycling routes he was a tad more forthcoming, advising me that because my intention was to cycle into Tavistock I should remain on the A386. He informed me even though the road was classed as an 'A' road, during weekdays, and out of peak-time, the traffic would be light, and due to the overnight and ongoing rain, the going would be far easier than the very hilly and muddy branch-section of the NCR 27 which ran into Tavistock. Thanking Callan, who was homeward bound and planning on having a lazy day in front of the goggle-box watching le Tour de France, I waved him off as he went right, leaving me to swing left and head up-hill past Lynford Gorge.

As I puffed and panted, I contemplated that, despite Le Tour being Fenella's and my favourite sporting event of the year, and the fact that we would be in France for most of its duration, it would be unlikely we'd see much of the action. I'd be cycling during the day and Fenella would be driving, and because we intended to camp most of the time, we'd most likely only have access to French radio during the evenings. Oh dear, I thought, to be so close, yet so far.

I was beginning to hit serious hill country. As I painfully trundled across the River Lyn, I could clearly make out the thundering water tumbling over the 100ft White Lady waterfall and the roar of the impressive Devils Cauldron, the natural wonders which dramatically bookend the one and half mile gorge.

I also noticed I was being shadowed by a police car. It had overtaken me about a mile before I reached the gorge, slowed down, then sped off, but it was back again driving the opposite way, slowing to obviously allow the occupant to eye me up and down. Halfway up the hill leading from the gorge, it again slowly overtook me to finally stop in a layby at the crest of the hill. As I slothfully approached, the driver got out of the car and did the world-over police officer movement, arm straight out, palm upwards, I was being instructed to stop. My mind began to race with dread, oh shit, now what have I gone and done? Then I remembered. I'd 'borrowed' a teaspoon from the breakfast table to eat my pot of fruit with later in the day. I could see it all, the papers would have a field day; 'The Great Teaspoon

Robbery' it would be called. I'd be hauled before the courts, found guilty as charged, incarcerated to find myself locked in a cell twenty-four-seven with Gavin the Giver who knew more about 'sharing' than I could ever imagine. I considered not stopping, but I got the idea if it came down to a chase along the country lanes I may find myself slightly disadvantaged trying to outpace a BMW motorway patrol car. I pulled to a standstill. The officer and I locked eyes. I decided to let him speak first in case I said the wrong thing and found myself in deeper trouble. 'Morning sir', he began, 'I saw you on the bike a few miles back, I thought about stopping you then, but thought I'd let you go on a bit further and top the hill, I hope you don't mind me stopping you now?'

Was his pleasantries just a ploy to get me to drop my guard I wondered? I'd better be careful in my replies, and hoping to immediately play the unconcerned card, I nonchalantly answered, 'oh yea.'

But I was unsure if my tactic had worked as he just gave a nod and began to circle me as I stood straddled-legged across my crossbar. 'It is your bike I presume sir?' came his sudden question.

Oh shit, is this what it's all about I internally cringed, it's not so much about teaspoons, he thinks I've nicked a bloody bike!

But before I could indignantly reply my innocence, he furthered, 'what a great looking bike, I love the colours. I've been wanting a Touring Pro for ages, I've been thinking about buying one and yours is the first I've actually seen, wow, I like it!' What's it like out on the road?

'Thank the Lord', was my first reaction, I won't be spending Christmas helping Gavin spread pleasure to all and sundry after all. What followed next was a chat between two cyclists about cycling, best rides, bikes, and Cube bikes in particular. Who would have thought that when a traffic cop pulls you over, like good mates the world over, you'd spend the next 20 minutes in friendly discussion about a shared passion?

According to the route maps I later looked at, the nine miles between Lynford and Tavistock were classed as being 'undulating'. If my poor old legs could have commented, I'm certain they'd have used a dissimilar, more Callan inspired Anglo Saxon based descriptive; let's just say I found the road to be frustratingly demanding. By the time I'd dropped into Tavistock and met Fenella I was more than ready to have a rest from pushing on the pedals for a while.

We located to Dukes Coffee House in the bustling Pannier Market and found a table outdoors to be served with wonderful dark roast coffee and jam scones, just what a tiring body needed. The term pannier market stems from when the goods to be sold were carried in large wicker baskets, or panniers, and many town markets originate from this practice. Tavistock's Pannier Market dates back to 1105 when Henry I gave a royal charter to the monks of St Mary and St Rumon Abbey allowing them to sell their bread products to the local populace. Of course nowadays hundreds of markets pop up countrywide selling every conceivable thing under the sun, but I surmise very few operate under a royal charter. I doubt the royals are too upset about this, they may even pop out of their palaces for a bit of hard bartering down at the local Sunday market-come-car-boot-sale. I can just picture old Philip hunting out the best value corgi-poo bags, while Charlie haggles over the price of King Edwards for Camilla's afternoon chip butty. No, I'm confident the House of Windsor aren't going to mind a touch of cash-in-hand market trader tax avoidance, why should they; just as long as all parties remember what Dennis Healey once commented, 'that the difference between tax avoidance and tax evasion is the thickness of the prison cell wall.' I wonder when it comes down to estimating the thickness of that taxing wall which of the parties will receive the most effective advice.

With Dukes being so popular and tables in short demand we were soon joined by another late breakfaster, Jim, a retired Scottish RAF Helicopter pilot who'd made his home in Tavistock after a career based at RMB Chivenor, the base I'd cycled past the day before. He was one of the heroic guys who'd risk their own lives to save others. He also had a much better turn of Scottish phrasing than Callan, commenting that the dismal weather was a 'huther of a day', meaning to be a day of intermittent showers. I could have listened to Jim's brogue over another good few coffees, but with time ticking and a ferry to catch we reluctantly bid him farewell, I pointed Pablo southwards, and climbing out of town I reacquainted myself with the NCR 27.

According to my route map, between Tavistock and Yelverton, near the village of Buckland Monachorum, the likelihood was that the woodland would be so muddy I'd find myself pushing Pablo for a mile or two. But having a Yorkshire sense of financial administration, when I'd bought my map in a fire sale, to save some cash, I'd bought an older edition, so it came as a pleasant surprise to discover a new tarmac cycle path complete with towering bridges spanning the muddy woods below. I'd call it parsimonious fortitude on my part, most of my friends would just say I was a lucky stingy sod.

Stopping on one of the bridges to gaze at the scenery below, from where I rested, looking forwards it was obvious the path was beginning to perceptibly rise. Commenting about this to a passing dog walker I was gruffly informed, 'that's nothing mate, wait until you get off the bridge and into the trees, then you'll know about it'. Not the most cheering of thoughts, I thought. But boy oh boy was she right. The path crossing the bridge ended in a squeeze-through style, and after ungainly squashing myself through, the gradient rose so sharply I had all on getting back on my bike and beginning to pedal. But I was determined not to let the hill beat me into submission, so winded, wheezing and wobbling I climbed through the last of the trees and into the open moorland of Dartmoor.

Crimson faced, as I came to a dismount at the crest of the hill, a fellow cyclist heading in the opposite direction asked if I was ok and did I need any help? Panting my thanks, and informing him I was just a little out of breath and would be fine in a minute or so, I pondered on the uncomfortable fact that that wasn't the first time that strangers had been concerned about me following my pathetic efforts at hill climbing. I must be in a right state, I reflected. If I couldn't make it up the incline of a Devonshire cycle path without looking like I needed the back-up of a personal paramedic, I asked myself, how the hell was I going to manage to pedal my way across the contours of the Pyrenees between France and Spain?

From my lofty perch, gazing into the stunning pallet of Dartmoor stretching towards the far horizon, and letting that worrying question bounce around my poor old nonce, another sensation began to impede my musings, why did the area around my crotch feel so peculiar? Looking, I was stunned to discover the answer; I appeared to have a horse attached to the front of my shorts! Admittedly it wasn't a big horse as horses go, but nevertheless it had somehow snook up to take me by complete surprise. It was a young Dartmoor pony, sticking his nose where it shouldn't, in the hope of having a chomp on the padding of my cycle shorts. Yelping in surprise, and fearful for certain parts of my anatomy, I roughly pushed its head away, only to deflect it onto Pablo's front wheel where the bloody thing tried to get its teeth into his tyre. I yanked Pablo's wheel from its grinding maw only to find the crazy beast trying to shove its head into my bike bag, presumably to have a go at my day's rations! Luckily it was zipped shut, giving me time to give the demonic mini-horse a sharp smack on its rear end. It did the trick, but as it raised its head to give me a malicious stare, of what I swear was pure malice, I got the feeling if I hung around much longer it'd be yowing for its buddies and they'd soon be getting their teeth into more than my shorts padding. I grabbed Pablo and was pedalling towards Yelverton as fast as my breathless body would allow. But at least it had stopped raining.

I knew Yelverton from old, it was the village where my LEJOG route and my La Vélodyssée crossed paths. Often called the 'gateway to Dartmoor' it was a favourite place for hordes of cyclists to begin and finish their jaunts into the delights offered by the bleak, yet spectacular moorland.

That Monday afternoon was no exception, and as I began to cross the village green I found myself surrounded by a large group of school kids out on an organised ride onto the moors. Lucky young beggars. My school outings were usually trips to some other school, or an afternoon spent in a museum full of glass encased bits of smashed pottery and broken Roman paving. Although I vividly remember one 3 day visit to Pateley Bridge in the Yorkshire Dales, not for the scenery, or the tramping up and down hills, but for the night my mate Lawrence, wanting to discover what was causing our teachers merriment, climbed out of the bedroom window, dropped down to land on a 500 gallon central heating oil tank and promptly fell through the rusting top and into the oil. Of course the rest of us had to quickly follow suit in order to pull him from the tank before he drowned. Just as we hauled him back through the window the teaching staff bundled into our bunk room demanding to know what on earth was going on. Ignoring Lawrence, who stood in the middle of the room dripping diesel from head to foot, one of our eagle eyed 'betters' looked out, saw the damage and demanded to know who had been 'swimming' in the tank. The question posed a moral dilemma; in our strict Catholic School it was considered a grievous sin to tell a lie, while in the upper 5th it was also considered cowardly and morally wanting to 'sprag' on a fellow classmate. So each of us in turn when asked, as etiquette demanded, took the Fifth Amendment and refused to answer. Lawrence was never asked. So for our insolence we all got our arses tanned. All that is except Lawrence who was told to go and get himself de-oiled. I never got to ride my bike as a school activity, a good job really, goodness knows what sort of bother Lawrence would have gotten himself and the rest of us into.

Fenella was also to be found at Yelverton and we managed a quick coffee together and agreed to meet up in Plymouth at the cities Go Outdoors store as we still had to buy ourselves a couple of camping chairs, other outdoor activity stores are available, but none offer Go Outdoors Caravan & Camping Club discount.

My run-in to Plymouth was a wonderful 13 mile downhill freewheel along the Plym Valley Railway Track, which parallels the immensely busy A386 trunk road.

Strangely, at the end of the track I came to a series of local cycle signs with all the details missing. As I stood looking in what must have been obvious confusion, a local commuting cyclist asked me where I was heading, and he told me to use the track that had the River Plym on the right and keep riding until I met The Laira Bridge, and then after crossing the bridge I would find the Go Outdoors store on my left. He was bang on with his directions, and I even managed to arrive before Fenella.

We soon bought a pair of folding chairs that offered a decent degree of comfort and we made it to the ferry port with plenty of time to spare, allowing us time to get an evening meal before departure. We ate at the Dock Café, both ordering their Classic Burgers, with Fenella choosing her favourite Jacobs Creek dry white wine, while I rehydrated with a couple of welcome pints of Doombar Ale.

Waiting to embark I got talking to an Aussie motorcyclist who was heading across the Channel to make his way towards Athens. He noticed me sipping my Torq Recovery and wondered if water and fresh fruit would do the same job. He could've been right, but as I'd made the decision to embrace a more scientifically based approach to bodily maintenance, and ignoring the fact that I'd began my recovery with a good few slurps of beer, I sipped my Torq with the determined anticipation of an ache free body the following morning.

The ferry departed on time and dozing in my bunk, listening to the swish of the sea far below our cabin, I mulled over my trip across Devon. All in all it had been relatively less taxing than I'd expected. I'd begun on cycling routes on which I'd journeyed before and that had been to my advantage helping me relax and giving me the chance of getting the 'feel' of my new bike. I also believed I'd given joy, or more likely bemused amusement, to other trail users with my tuneless attempts at removing my feet from my pedals, admittedly an issue which during my preparations I'd given little thought about, but one which had nearly cost me dearly on the platform at Great Torrington. I hadn't got lost in the traditional sense, although for a good few miles I had to concede I was unsure whether I was on the correct roads or not. Two thirds of the route had been hilly, mostly of the up kind, but the track was considerably better surfaced than I had imagined. I'd been slow, but had managed to top all the hills without walking, and the final section had been a superb downhill bonus. I had met two Scots with contrasting verbal skills, plus a uniformed Cube enthusiast, and we'd made the ferry with time to spare.

All alone on the Tarka Trail heading to
Fremington Quay looking back
towards Barnstable

Part 2

Biking Brittany – A Whiter Shade of Pale (Procol Harum)

When we awoke we were in French waters approaching Roscoff. We'd both slept extremely well. I usually do on ferries. Maybe it's the gentle vibrations of the turbines combined with the rhythmic rock of the hull that lull me into slumber. Thankfully, the ointment Fenella had managed to get in Tavistock was beginning to do its job and her midge bites were already looking much better. We had time to join the other passengers for a slurp of strong coffee and for me to crumble a couple of croissants down the front of my shirt, then it was down to the car deck to be ready with the other drivers for unloading. It was the usual organised chaos as we queued for passport control, though fortunately there weren't too many drivers of German cars selfishly pushing their way to the front of the queue. Although I suppose it's possible to understand why many drivers of these cars drive so aggressively to the frustration of other people; imagine spending all that money on huge new Mercedes, Audi or BMW and then after collecting your gleaming new car from the showroom at the first roundabout you come to discovering that it doesn't come equipped with any indicators. I'd be peeved too.

Exiting the dock area the task was to locate La Vélodyssée track itself. I had a rough idea of its location relative to the port and turning left we drove all of 200 metres before spotting a cycle track crossing a small roundabout directly in front. Was that it? As easy as that? I was willing to give it a try.

Already kitted out in my cycling gear, and after quickly unloading Pablo, securing my handlebar bag containing my phone and route cards and my rear bag with a few nibbles, spare inner tube, pump, tools and an extra bidon, after all the months of waiting and worry, I was about to start the 1,200km of the French sections of La Vélodyssée, arguably one of Europe's most prestigious cycle routes. My La Vélodyssée route booklet, Le Routard, is broken down into 12 sections (unlike La Vélodyssée website which shows 14 sections), with each section having a number ètapes (short sectors), but I imagined my whole journey to be in 6 larger segments. 1, Devon (which I'd already cycled), 2, Brittany, 3, Pays de la Loire, 4, Poitou-Charentes, 5, Aquitaine, 6, the Pyrenean foothills and San Sebastián.

As I was preparing Pablo, Fenella began to sort her road maps so she could match them up with, Le Routard, which she would use while I used the copies of the route maps I'd made back at home. But she couldn't find it. Asking me where I'd put it, a dreadful realisation hit me. 'Well you know I wanted to keep it in a safe place,' I mumbled. 'Well I did, I put it safely on the bookshelf in the lounge. Trouble is I think it's still safe, I think it's still on the bookshelf at home'. Thankfully, as this situation proved, my life has been made so much easier, by; 1) Fenella rarely losing her rag, 2) Fenella, in times of tension being able to keep a clear head and think logically, 3) Fenella being organised in the midst of my disorganisation, 4) Fenella always seemingly to have a plan B, while I always seem to struggle fully understanding plan A, even when it was my plan in the first place, 5) Fenella……yes you've got it, my life has been made so much easier because of Fenella! She soon figured out she could photograph my copied cards with her mobile and use her phone instead of the booklet. Yet again I was saved.

Even after the stupidity of my forgetfulness, the situation seemed to be both a little unreal and bizarrely low-key. There I stood, 8.37am on a Tuesday morning, opposite four large green re-cycling skips, next to an abandoned Tabac, facing an inconsequential roundabout, on which an old lady was encouraging her tatty toy poodle to toilet by farting loudly, all the while muttering incoherently into a mobile phone. There was no official start line, no route signs, in fact no other cyclists, and I'd seen a few touring cyclists when leaving the ferry, so where were they all? Was I by myself in starting La Vélodyssée? Was I even on La Vélodyssée? There was only one way to find out. So with a peck on the cheek from Fenella and a promise to meet up near lunchtime, and a cheer from the old lady, not for me, for her dog who at last had managed to have a rancid smelling dump, I was away to begin my French adventures and La Vélodyssée Section 1 (76.6km).

When on previous cycle trips I'd always broken the journey down into daily stages and tried to stay faithfully as close to my schedule as possible, often causing me to suffer in the latter stages. But for my La Vélodyssée, apart from the Devonshire sections, where I'd had to make sure I finished in time to catch the ferry, I'd decided to adopt a much more relaxed approach. Therefore, I had no set daily finishes in mind, it would be down to how I felt on each particular day that would determine how far I cycled.

Getting Pablo rolling my non-goal for that day was to begin heading towards Morlaix where I hoped to meet Fenella for a late morning coffee, and then on to wherever during the afternoon. It was a gentle climb out of Roscoff and I soon found myself in the countryside, although not before I had had a brief excursion into someone's back garden after mistaking the passage running along the side of a house as the cycle track. The old couple working their veg patch did appear a little surprised by my visit, but they didn't say a great deal, but that could've been more down to their confusion as I rather mixed my linguistic apologies up by mumbling, 'oops, het spijt me, excuse moi.....er sorry'. But not to worry, at least following all the exasperating Brexit debates I was demonstrating a little European togetherness.

Crossing the D58, the road Fenella would have used to exit the Roscoff area, making my way along a muddied bridle way, I spotted my first French photo opportunity. Leaning against the decking of an abandoned barn, was an old sit-up-and-beg complete with bunches of onions draped from its handlebars. Without doubt a rather iconic touristy sight, but still, worth a snap or two I reckoned. About 3km later two French lads and one British lad came joyfully speeding past me on adapted road bikes. Wishing them good cycling I could only be jealous of their youthful exuberance, their obviously overflowing enthusiasm and most of all, their wind resistant profiles. I immediately felt old, weighty and slothful. Just on the outskirts of Morlaix, I came across them with one of their front tyres removed and the contents of a puncture repair kit spread untidily across the cycle way. Upon enquiring they assured me all was ok and they'd catch me later, it turned out to be much later than we all thought.

Morlaix was not as I expected. About 7km inland from the nearest inlet, my first sighting of the town was a mickle of large yacht masts, bobbing and swaying, set against the breath-taking backdrop of the foothills of the Monts d'Arrée Mountains, which themselves seem to be overshadowed by the town's magnificent 14 arched, 58 metre high, 292 metre long stone viaduct. Stopping in the port area, dismounting and drinking greedily from my bidon another sensation began to assault me, the heat. It was as if the town was directly sucking energy from the sun and presenting it to me as a gift for my stopover.

I found a shady place to stand Pablo while I had a wander along the quayside. From various information boards I discovered that Morlaix had once been the largest port in Brittany, making its wealth from specialising in the production and the trade of linen.

Nowadays, its largest income came from the likes of me in my guise as a tourist. However, within a short time of wandering in the lunchtime heat this transitory sightseer was soon found to be scuttling back into the safety of the shade where I'd left Pablo. Being on the bike I hadn't noticed just how hot it had become during the morning, perhaps this was because of the cooling breeze which always seems to accompany a bike rider.

Having heard from Fenella informing me she would shortly arrive in town, while I waited I took the opportunity to test out my engineering aptitudes by having a go at adjusting the tension of my SPD pedals. During the morning I'd again been persisting in trying to be comfortable and confident in my use of them. I was happy with my right side pedal, finding I could quickly lock and disengage my foot with ease, but no matter what 70's ditty I shimmied to I still wasn't confident with releasing my foot quickly from my left side pedal. I thought if I could adjust the left pedal tension to the same as the right I'd be ok. Using my hardly-used gleaming bike multi-tool I carefully unwound the left pedal tension grub screw to the same position as the right side, and crossing my fingers in the hope I'd done it correctly, I called it a day with regards to my masterly mechanical undertakings.

Fenella parked in the port car park, and a short stroll later we found a wonderfully shaded café in the old quarter where we re-energised with strong coffees and ham and cheese crépes'. I really fancied a long cool beer, but with the heat and still having an afternoon of cycling in front of me, I reluctantly resisted. Leaving Fenella to enjoy another coffee I reacquainted myself with the heat and said cheerio to Morlaix. However Morlaix didn't want to say bye-bye to me. It took me a good hour to re-locate La Vélodyssée, but not before I'd wobbled myself through several car parks, two office complexes, a school playground (thankfully empty of kids) and an underground section of a police station. No one said a dicky-bird to me, I guessed they must have thought, just another crazy Brit, let him get on with it and with luck we'll never have to see him again.

Dissecting the northern section of the Parc Naturel Régional d'Armorique, following the line of the rivers Le Jarlot and Le Squiriou, skirting villages including; Cosquer-Pinard, Keradraon, Kerdalidec and Kertanguy, the track out of Morlaix is a disused and adapted old railway line, much like the Trans Pennine Trail I'm so familiar with riding back home in Yorkshire. All, that is, except the smells and rubbish free condition. Unlike Britain, the aromas I detected as I tootled along weren't the dusty and grubby reek of nearby factories and warehousing complexes that border so many of the British cycle-ways. Instead I could breathe in the aromatic mixture of fruits, flowers, freshly cropped cereal crops and ripening corn. Also, as I passed under bridged roadways it was so refreshing not to discover piles of dumped masonry, broken microwaves, yawning rusty fridges, shattered TV's and mounds of tattered and rotting clothing, which a small percentage, of brainless and socially ignorant British 'scum' seem more than happy to decorate our once beautiful countryside with. Little do they realise in their pathetic and filthy need to clear their own environments, if their mess were not cleared up by other caring folk, their masses of shit would eventually reach back to their own doorsteps. Earlier in the year, I read with amusement that a Yorkshire farmer, completely stalled with a local cowboy builder dumping rubbish on his land, and knowing where the guy lived, one night loaded his tractor-trailer unit with a couple of tons of 'ripening' manure and dumped the whole lot on the builders driveway and front garden.

Despite the omission of scrap, I wasn't alone on La Vélodyssée , as in Devon, a school party were out enjoying the freedoms of the trail, although this group was younger than their English cousins. I felt for one chap, small and rather rounded in deportment he was riding a diminutive mountain bike and he was finding the hilly terrain difficult. Still, he was determined in attitude and he kept surging ahead of me on downhills, only for me to overtake him again as the elevation rose. I could tell from his teachers face he wasn't relishing being this little chaps trailing chaperone, but hey, we can't all be cycling superstars. The great thing about being on a bike is the bike's not at all bothered how fast you ride it, neither are the surroundings you ride in, or the majority of other cyclists, particularly tourers and leisure cyclists. It's all about getting out there, the enjoyment of it, the fresh air and if lucky arriving at your chosen destination; and for me....never ever the speed. I'm glad to report the little chap got there in the end, he finished his ride at the same point as I ended my first day cycling on French soil, on the outskirts of Scrignac.

However, no matter how fast or slow I would have liked to cycle on that particular day, and well before my finish at Scrignac, I'd once again had bother with my pedals. Not the tricky problem of unlocking my feet from my left pedal, I'd solved that difficulty once and for all, I wouldn't have to worry about unlocking my left foot ever again. It seemed my meticulous skills in mechanics earlier in the day hadn't been so hot after all, somehow in my clumsiness I'd released the left pedal tension screw so enthusiastically that it was no longer there, it had fallen out somewhere along the track. Therefore, the SDP side of my left pedal was useless, from that point onwards I had to use the 'comfort' side of my pedals only. Well at least it had saved me the embarrassment of trying to remember anymore dreadful 70's singalong tunes!

Our campsite for the night was La Riviere d'Argent, a few miles from La Vélodyssée, so it meant loading Pablo on the car for the drive. While I did this I was again struck by the heat once I'd stopped cycling. I'd expected the heat to be intense in, and towards southern France, but we'd only hopped over the Channel, travelled about 60km and seemingly the temperature had risen over 15°C, it didn't bode well for my journey southwards.

Complete with small bar, shop and open air and indoor swimming pools, set in forestry land, La Riviere d'Argent was a great little hideaway of a campsite, and following my day on the bike I was more than ready for a beer and a dip in the pool, in fact I could've leapt in while still dressed for cycling. But we had a job to do before we could enjoy beer and swimming, set up camp. This was the first time we'd had a go at putting the tent up since our initial try-out after purchasing. Having inflatable tubing instead of poles, despite a bit of puffing and panting, in less than 10 minutes, we had a fully erected tent, sleeping compartment and inflated double air bed. Not bad for a first time we thought. Then it was swim and beer time. There were a few other campers on site, Dutch from their vehicle markings, but we had the pool to ourselves and so too the outdoor bar area.

Our evening meal consisted of a one-pan concoction of tinned ravioli, a freshly baked baguette and a bottle of local produced Muscadet from the Chon Gilbert et Fils vineyard. In spite of the heat of the day still clinging on in the tent well after dark, I didn't take much rocking before I fell into a deep sleep. All in all not a bad introduction to France I mused.

Following such an agreeable first day, I began day two feeling rather deflated; during the night our airbed had sprung a leak and we awoke laying with only its flattened profile and the tent floor between us and the unyielding sun-baked ground. Funny how I hadn't noticed the tree roots under the tent the night before, it's illuminating what a tender bum can inform about the terrain!

Breakfast was cereals, jam and a baguette and as much tea as my tummy could take. Then it was de-camp and a drive back to my previous day's finish point at the deserted Gite d'Étape De La Gare. The tent was just as easy to take down as put up, with the additional pleasure of enjoying the booming sound of the sudden release of air from the air-frame as the valves were opened. Although, I'm not sure the other campers appreciated our early morning clamouring's as much as we did.

Back at La Gare, even so early in the day, it was obvious it was going to be just as warm, if not warmer than the day before. Unloading Pablo I spotted another touring cyclist, who had been camping on the trail, packing his tent away and I couldn't help wondering in that heat how he had managed to remain sufficiently hydrated with no water points nearby, no shops or houses and him seemingly not to have any other water containers other than a single bidon on his bike. I hoped he was going to be ok during the day.

Heading towards the south west, I was aiming to meet the Brest/Nantes Canal, which over the coming days I hoped to follow for a fair few miles. A strange sensation I would have to get used to was that no matter which actual direction I would be traveling in, the manner in which my route cards were printed would indicate that I was either cycling directly eastwards or westwards. Therefore, despite the reality of my mornings south/westerly progress, as I looked at my mapping it was easy to be visually duped into thinking I was cycling towards the east.

Skirting the villagers of St Ambroise and Kerrolland I was cycling the edges of Finstere, a region of Brittany famed for its Breton mythology. According to local folklore it was in the lands of Finstere that Ankou, the personification of death, wandered about with his cart near Yuen Ellés, the gates of Hell, collecting the lost souls of goblins, elves, leprechauns and korrigans to transport through the gates. Thankfully, as I passed by it must have been old Ankou's day off because of the unusual hot weather and I wondered whether in his rush to get home he'd left his gates slightly ajar. But who knows, it could have been less Finstere folklore and instead Brittany as a whole suffering from one of those uncomfortably meteorological freakish bouts of searing weather.

I joined the Brest/Nantes canal in the town of Carhaix Plouguer, where I'd arranged to meet Fenella for coffee and cake. Located in the region of Poher, bordered by the Arreé Mountains in the north and the Black

Mountains in the south, Carhaix sits on a natural plateaux 140 metres above sea level. When under Roman occupation the occupiers had discovered it to be an ideal topographic place to construct a 27km aqueduct to provide water to the ancient city of Vorgium. The aqueduct was originally fed by the stream of Madeleine, which route was later utilised when constructing the Brest/Nantes canal.

Given Carhaix's spectacular historical constructions and ties to the past glories of an expansive and all powerful empire of trade and cultural dominance, it seemed fitting that myself and Fenella should meet up in one of France's ever expanding empires of commerce and persuasive social domination, a sprawling E.Leclerc hypermarket. Arriving slightly before Fenella, locking Pablo in the cycle park, I couldn't help noticing two other bikes loaded for touring, especially when one of them was a well-used British built Carlton Randonneur. Had I met my first La Vélodysséeres?

It felt so pleasing to get out of the days heat and into the revitalizing chill of the hypermarket's air conditioning. While I waited for Fenella I had a chance to search out if E.Leclerc had any air beds we could purchase to save further nights of grounded repose. Luckily they did, and after collecting the most luxuriously substantial inflatable mattress I could obtain, spotting Fenella arrive, I found a tranquil spot in the café and ordering coffees, iced Orangina's for both of us, and a selection of gooey cakes for myself, I settled down to my sickly sweet lunch. However, I couldn't spot any other cyclists in the café, British or otherwise, maybe they too were shopping for sugary goodies somewhere in the store. Not to worry I mused, if they were heading in the same direction as me maybe I'd be able to meet up with them later, it would be good to have a natter with some fellow two wheeled travellers.

Relaxing over our coffees, catching up with Fenella's morning and deciding upon a campsite for the night, I had a chance to swap my route cards, as Carhaix was the final destination of Section 1 of La Vélodyssée. But with it being lunchtime, and feeling relatively fresh in the legs, despite the intensifying heat, it wasn't a difficult choice for me to decide to cycle further into the afternoon and begin Section 2 (86.4km). Yet it somehow felt strange for me to be beginning another section at mid-day. During all my other solo tours I'd always ensured that I'd completed a set section before finishing for the day. But because La Vélodyssée was pre-planned, and mileage-wise each section differed widely, it meant occasionally it would be necessary for me to finish and start sections of La Vélodyssée at differing times of the day.

Back out in the heat of the day at the start of La Vélodyssée Section 2 (113km) and with Pablo loaded with a couple of extra litres of water, I noticed the two touring bikes had gone, hopefully in the same direction as me I mused, it would be good to have a natter with some fellow travellers. It was a bit of a tug from the hypermarket to the canal, which came as a surprise, it seemed unusual to go uphill towards such a body of water.

Once on the towpath I immediately came across four cyclists going in the opposite direction. Two of the quartet were lugging trailers, one trailer was loaded with camping gear, the other trailer with three young children, but the most noticeable thing about them was their speed, they were fair bombing along. 'Great', I thought, 'this looks good, if they can hit those speeds lumping all that stuff and three kids to boot, well I should be able to get some really good speeds going'. But I couldn't, and approaching a lock I was finding the going challenging. Then it dawned on me. In my naivety I'd presumed the canal would run on a level, but of course it had to follow the lay of the land, hence the lock, hence the speed of the other cyclists, they were going downhill while I was still going uphill. This fact was reinforced by the sheer number of locks I passed in such a short number of kilometres, in a distance of about 10km I gave up counting at 25, where in actuality there must have been more than double that number.

Leading to the village of Tronjoly the well maintained towpath surface became covered in a thick layer of loose small white stones, it was like trying to cycle on marbles, not the most confidence building sensation when balancing on two wheels along the side of deep water. With the heat I was dripping sweat, and as the dust from the stones began to cling to me I slowly began to resemble Fred the Homepride-man, the rotund bowler hatted guy from an old TV baking advert, not the most dynamic of superheroes, less cape and heroics, more pinny and self-raising flour. At the outskirts of the village I discovered the reason for the re-surfacing, a new road bridge was being built across the canal. The stones had been laid to protect the track from the damage that could be caused from a fleet of small trucks which were being used to transport materials from a store adjacent to the construction site. The construction also resulted in a diversion off the towpath and into the dappled foliage of woodland bordering the canal, providing me a welcome break from the scorching sunshine.

Rounding a bend I nearly collided with two cyclists plodding along at a snail's pace, they were riding the bikes that had been locked outside E.Leclerc, and they were British. I slowed to match their sedate pace and to have a natter, but firstly, because of their slowness I asked if they were ok, the woman of the two mumbled something inaudible and gave a brief nod, but with a huge grin the chap informed me all was fine. As we cycled he told me they too had set off from Roscoff four days ago, and were making their way to Redon, which was also on my schedule. As we nattered, complaining about the heat, enthusing about the quality and the beauty of La Vélodyssée I realised the chap and I were leaving his partner behind. I began slowing to allow her to catch us up, but he didn't seem to want her to and he kept pedalling at the same pace and talking over his shoulder in an effort for me to catch him instead, all the while she dropped further and further behind. I began to have the embarrassing experience of being piggy in the middle of what was dawning on me was obviously a couple in the midst of some sort of disagreement. Eventually, the woman stopped altogether leaving us to continue onward, but about a kilometre later the chap pulled hard on his brakes and blurted out, 'oh bollocks to this, it's like riding with a dressmaker's dummy, I may as well talk to my bloody bike, she's driving me mad!' I was lost for words, but I knew there was no way I was getting myself stuck in the middle of their problems and acting as some type of two wheeled mediator. However, before I could reply he apologised for his outburst and turned to make his way back to his partner. Which made me think, just as cyclists come in all shapes and sizes, they too must bring with them all types of tempers, tantrums and temperaments.

Approaching the town of Rostrenen another diversion directed me off the temporary diversion, taking me beyond the boundaries of my route card. I managed to follow this secondary deviation for a few kilometres but in the end lost the signs altogether. Finding a rutted muddied track leading roughly in the direction of where I thought the town and canal could be, and deciding to take fate in my hands I gave it a try. It nearly proved to be a fateful decision, particularly when the track led me across the bottom of a farmer's field where an angry looking bullock slowly began to stalk me and give me the type of stare I'd last seen in a Terminator movie. But on making it across the field in one piece, lumping Pablo through a small gate and closing it firmly against my four legged foe, I couldn't help but give the beast a steely stare and snarl, 'I won't be back!'

Rostrenen seemed to be deserted, apart from a scraggy looking dog which was laying on the hot concrete roadway licking its nether's with the manic glee only an ill-disposed canine psychopath can administer. Not the most auspicious of welcoming's to the town I thought at the time, but as events unfolded, perhaps one sufficiently suitable.

As well as not seeing any people in and about Rostrenen neither could I spot any signs for La Vélodyssée, or the canal. I traversed a number of streets, but to no avail. I began to suspect either the canal had disappeared or I was lost. Noticing a Tabac, propping Pablo to wait in the sun, I shouldered myself through the half-opened doorway. You know the scene in many a western where the tall lean heroic stranger in town enters the saloon and all noise stops, all inside turn to stare at him, while his eyes glint with a steely stare of unconcerned assurance and he mutters some wise-crack, saunters unfazed to the bar, and in a dark brown cheroot hardened voice confidently demands, 'whisky'. Well I had a similar experience. The bar was dark and dingy inside with about a dozen patrons sat at small triangular wooden tables all staring transfixed to a small TV playing shrilly above the bar, behind which stood who I took to be the proprietor pouring greenish coloured liquid into a well-polished spirit glass. Not only did all talking suddenly cease and all eyes turn my way, finishing his pouring, the proprietor reached upwards and with a sharp snap turned off the TV. Then just to top things off nicely what should squeeze past me and enter this den of inhospitality but the damned dog with his saliva slobbered knackers. No heroic wise-crack from me, no confident saunter to the bar to subdue the antagonistic locals to my resolute will, instead, without a peep I slowly backed my way out of the doorway, retrieved Pablo and peddled off pretty sharpish.

Pulling to a stop about half a kilometre later, I wondered if what I believed had happened had in fact actually occurred. Had I imagined it due to a combination of exhaustion and dehydration? Or had I misread the local's hostility when in fact they were being attentively welcoming to my arrival. I'll never know, I never went back to find out.

Just to augment the peculiar, upon leaving the perimeter of Rostrenen I came across a narrow metalled lane which led me over a rickety footbridge and back to the canal towpath. It seemed to me that for some inexplicable reason the canal had mysteriously bypassed the town. As I cycled towards Gouarec, where we'd identified a campsite to stay for the night, I still couldn't help thinking about my encounter back in the Tabac, it felt as if I'd briefly wandered through a parallel universe, less like a 1950's western film and more like a happening in the X Files; all very Moulder and Skully.

Following my encounter with the paranormal I realised apart from a small cake at lunchtime I hadn't eaten all day, I'd gone through several bidons of Science in Sport

(SIS) hydration fluids and chewed on a couple of energy jellies, but nothing solid. On saying that, when I found a small shelter to hide away from the sun to begin my rations, all it amounted to was more water and a selection of fruit and nuts, which over the past days had been my usual fare when cycling. I was finding, due to my continuing heat induced dehydration, eating in bulk had become near impossible. When cycling I didn't feel the need for food, I was just guzzling as much liquid as I could. I knew if my friends and fellow cyclists had known of this they would have been berating me big time via social networking, so I kept mum and remained faithful to my liquid based diet.

According to its web-site Camping De Gouarec claims to be, 'the most beautiful campsite on the Nantes/Brest Canal...' As I approached from the far bank it certainly looked that way, an oasis of greenery, complete with the odd splash of orange, red and blue from the tents dotted randomly about its acreage. Fenella had arrived before me and God bless her she had found a secluded spot and had all the camping gear already unpacked. We soon had our camp up and running and before showering we decided to have a couple of cold beers bought from the campsite and to sit at the shaded tables next to the office. The site was run by an English family who professed to offer simple friendly family run camping, 1960's style. Looking at the other campers it was apparent that most were cyclists either on tour or using hired bikes from the campsite. We could see an elderly couple who appeared to be on tour, carrying all their gear in a bike trailer along with a medium sized dog. Another younger couple, this time with a child trailer and a rather large German shepherd. A solitary chap about my age in his one man tent and like me, riding a Cube Touring bike, and as we sipped our beers, another touring cyclist entered the campsite, propped his bike near to us and introduced himself to be Filip from Varberg in Western Sweden. Interestingly Filip told us that he was on his way back to Sweden and had been navigating his way by using a GPS unit similar to my, as yet, unused model, but it had fallen from his bike and broken. However, he had called in a village bike shop whose mechanic had rigged a coupling lead from his front wheel dynamo to power a small iPad on which he could run Google Mapping, clever or what?

Finishing our beers it was shower time, entering the shower block I began to fully comprehend the 1960's theme of the campsite. The shower cubicles looked as if they'd last seen any cleaning materials when Procol Harum were at number 1 in July 1967 with ' A Whiter Shade of Pale', which was ironic to say the least. The showers were absolutely filthy and what colour could be seen was nowhere near a shade of white, it was more like mottled brown with the odd hint of evil yellowish peeping through. Despite me not being at my most polished and still covered from head to toe with an unflattering sheen of white stone dust, looking at the state of the showers I had the impression if I used one I'd exit grubbier then when I went in. Therefore, I resorted to what my old Mum would have called a 'cold flannel bath', not the choice of body launderings following a hot day in the saddle, but probably a damn sight healthier then the risk of succumbing to Legionaries' Disease from having a shower.

Supper consisted of camp cooked Spaghetti Bolognese, crusty baguettes and a bottle of local red, and once again we used the provided tables and chairs in the office structure on which to eat our meal. While we were eating we noticed another pair of cyclists enter the site, quickly erect a couple of one man tents and wander over to eat at the adjacent table, this was Andy and Elvis (no, I'm not kidding), who were on a one night stopover making their way to St Malo for the ferry back to blighty. Naturally we got talking. Andy and Elvis were on a week-long circular trip of Brittany and like all other cyclist I'd met they'd been amazed by the wonderful cycling the region had to offer and mightily surprised by the unusual heat. They were also slightly jealous of my plans to head towards Spain and immensely jealous that Fenella, who they saw as nothing less than saintly, should be so kind and helpful towards me, both saying their wives wouldn't even consider entertaining such an idea, let alone executing it. Which leads me to say, they are right, I'm one lucky man to have such a wonderful life-buddy. Andy went further and made a note of my Facebook Blog and JustGiving sites and told me on his arrival home he would begin to follow my progress southwards and make a donation to my charity. Andy was true to his word and added the following to my JustGiving site:

Mike and your lovely wife ---best of luck with your efforts and hope you have a fair wind!!! Best wishes Andy Young ---we met at campsite Gouarec.

Thanks Andy, you're a star!

Unfortunately, because of their tight schedule, Andy and Elvis couldn't stay chatting for too long, they were planning an early start in the morning and had to retire to get some well-needed sleep. As they left, with both of us in agreement about what fine folk they were, I couldn't help exclaiming, 'well at least we can both say we were there when Elvis left the building'.

Back at our tent, watching the sun set over the canal I reflected that despite the 1960's campsite not being up to a July 1967 No. 1 standard, at least with my preternatural confrontation in the Tabac bar in Rostrenen, I could symbolise with the affair with another two songs from that same year, 'Strange Brew', by Cream, and, 'The Happening', by the Supremes.

Unlike me, the sun was burning with enthused energy when we emerged from our tent at about 7am. The temperature was already hitting the high 20's and the shades of the previous evening had been replaced by a glaring morning brightness. Andy and Elvis had already decamped and departed and most of the other campers were up and about. The couple with the dog had their tent down and loaded in their cycle trailer ready for the off. The solo cyclist was just exiting the campsite on his Cube, and the couple with the German shepherd were also in the process of leaving, although their tent was still standing. It appeared that even at that ungodly hour of the day Fenella and I were the sleepy-heads of the crew.

We breakfasted on what had become our usual first meal of the day, cereals and the remains of a previous night's baguette laced with copious amounts of jam to improve its dryness, and lashings of hot tea. Like the German shepherd owners, we too were leaving the tent erected, allowing me to use the site as a base for another days cycling, meeting Fenella wherever I finished, and then returning there later. We thought that without having the need to de-camp and re-pack the car I would be able to speed up my morning's departure. It would also give Fenella the opportunity of having a bit of a lazy day, allowing her to catch up with her reading and being able to have a nose around Gouarec village. After liberally applying my factor 50 sun cream, my familiar day's rations and even more drinkables packed aboard Pablo, with sleep still partly clouding my sunglasses shielded eyes, I wobbled my way out of Camping De Gouarec to sluggishly trail after my fervently ever-ready fellow cyclists.

I thought I was in for an easy day of navigation, all I had to do was keep the canal on one side or the other, it seemed to be so simple, and so it turned out to be, at least for the first 5km. But arriving at the hamlet of La Villeneuve I came across a warning sign informing me that somewhere in the nearby vicinity the towpath was partially obstructed due to 'industrialisation', and it recommended that I follow the 'alternative' deviation signs. Initially, these led me onto the busy D5, under a tall viaduct, across the humming N164, and about 8km uphill towards the larger town of Laniscat. Cursing under my breath about diversions, and about how each damn diversion seemed to take me uphill, I wearily wobbled my way upwards until I reached the outskirts of Laniscat, but for the life of me I couldn't spot any further signs. Turning tail, I freewheeled back downhill all the while keeping my eyes peeled for any elusive signs, but to no avail. However, on the way back down I noticed several people peering over the edge of the viaduct, and one chap wearing a bright yellow coat waved greetings my way. I wondered if the viaduct was the alternative route, but it was at least 80ft above the roadway and despite looking around I couldn't see any way of getting myself, let alone Pablo up, so I dismissed the idea. Never mind an alternative route I profaned, I saw no other alternative other than to make my way back to the towpath. I then thought to follow it until I met whatever industrialisation hindered my way, and hoping at that juncture I would find a way around it, or at least an alternative, alternative cycleway that was accurately signposted.

Back alongside the canal I had the towpath all to myself. I guessed all the other users had searched more effectively than I had, and that they had found, and taken the diversion. 7km later I discovered why they had bothered, and also, just what the term industrialisation meant. I came to a large stone quarry which had collapsed and thrown large lumps of rock all the way across the towpath. The path wasn't partially obstructed; as far as the eye could see it was completely blocked and totally impassable. Although luckily the canal itself appeared to be clear of any rubble, the tumbling boulders had ceased their movements at the water's edge where a strong steel fence had been erected, presumably in case of such an occurrence.

I didn't have to cycle all the way back down the canal side, the quarry had a concrete service road which opened out on to the towpath. It appeared that I'd found my alternative, alternate diversion, although I still couldn't spot any signposts. Unfortunately the road had such an uphill gradient, 14% in places, with the sun viscously reflecting off the bright concrete surface and slamming into my being, I was soon so dripping in perspiration I reckoned if I'd tried to swim around the blockage instead, I'd have been no wetter. Although it's fair to say, with the need to carry Pablo on my back I probably would have drowned. Which I guess, is why in triathlons the athletes are allowed to swim without their bikes. Although, the way TV companies compete to make the most provocative programmes possible, in the future who knows what Ant and Dec will be presenting next?

Other issues about the road which were bothering me were its direction and its shape. It was nowhere near straight, rather semi-circular, and even more worryingly curving northwards. This was annoyingly confirmed when I reached the small village of Rosquelfen. Not that the village was annoying in any way, in fact it appeared to be a beautifully and well cared for little place. The sort of community that is often depicted on the lids of jigsaw boxes that harp back to the 1950's. In which the makers of these puzzles would like us to believe that the world was a much more respectful and peaceful place in which to live, all quietude and social harmony. Interestingly, I've never come across a jigsaw picture that shows the dirt encrusted poverty of the times, the clearing of the back-to-back slums and the hurried construction of the socially isolating concrete high rises. No, the annoying thing about Rosquelfen was it was situated alongside the D5, nestling under the shadow of the towering viaduct. I'd ended up about 200 metres away from where I'd originally become diverted from La Vélodyssée. Not only had I got myself lost, I had managed to get myself lost twice in the same place!

I had no option but to give up on La Vélodyssée track and follow the road system to the town of Mûr-de-Bretagne and hope that once there I would be able to reacquaint myself with the trail. It didn't prove to be so straightforward. I made it to Mûr-de-Bretagne with ease, I even got myself on the trail, the trouble was it was the wrong trail. But I only discovered that when some 2 hours later I pedalled into the town square of Cleguérec, a town some 20km west of Pontivy, where I had arranged to meet Fenella. It was time for me to admit defeat and ask for help. Which of course meant me phoning Fenella to come and rescue me from my own stupidity, something I hate to confess she has been doing on a regular basis for the last 40 years.

While I waited, hiding from the piercing sun under the shade of a tree, on a patch of seared grass along the edge of a Super U car park, I thought at least we'll be able to buy ourselves some snacks and chilled drinks for lunch. But to add insult to injury, before Fenella arrived the supermarket's doors were locked to the public, no doubt to allow the staff to enjoy a long leisurely lunch of their own. 'Selfish bastards', I couldn't help but curse to the red ants that had decided to come out of their nest to run up and down my legs, presumably just to make my day a tad more uncomfortable. 'What had happened to the customer comes first theory of shop keeping', I fumed, while I leapt around the tree like a crazed crossed stringed puppet, all the while trying to clear my legs of their company, 'I bet that wouldn't have happened back in jigsaw land'. 'Arhhh!'

I was still muttering and cursing when Fenella arrived, but at least I managed to get some relatively cool water into me from the car cool box and give myself a welcome swill down. Fenella, of course, was all calm and reason and she soon had me delivered back to the towpath at the narrow road bridge at Kergicquel, and once more heading towards Pontivy.

Where the River Blavet meets the Brest/Nantes canal, according to legend, Pontivy was originally founded by Ivy, an English monk who constructed a wooden bridge across the River Blavet, hence Pont d'Ivy. Whatever the truth about its founding the town quickly developed to become one of Brittany's major seats of power and influence, and later became one of Napoleon Bonaparte's 'new towns', and an important military centre.

Most-all was at peace as I crossed the river and met Fenella on the outskirts of Pontivy. I use the term 'most-all', because due to the combinations of my unintended wanderlust, being locked away from much needed cold refreshments and the sizzling heat, I suspected my blood pressure was in a state of bubbling turmoil. When my mind's eye pictured the legendary good monk Ivy, I imagined him to be the personification of serenity and habit clad harmony, he certainly wouldn't have been out of place calmly displaying his carpentry skills on the lid of my imaginary jigsaw box. Whereas for anyone watching me enter town, and were asked to give me a monkish comparable, they'd have more associated me with that mad, bad, and seemingly permanently 'lost it', Rasputin the Demented. It was fair to reflect I was not a contented bunny.

Pontivy is the end of La Vélodyssée Section 2, and it was obviously time for me to call it a day before I really blew my cool, or at least what bit of cool I had left. It wasn't just too hot for me of course, Fenella had had enough as well. Although her car had climate control that was only of use when she was driving, at other times she had the same problem as me, how to hide away from the heat of the day. She told me she'd managed as best as she could, parking her car under the shading of trees when opportune, but in Pontivy she had no option but to park alongside the river and wait for my arrival sitting on a bench offering only partial shade. For two folk more used to the temperatures offered by the climate of South Yorkshire, usually alternating between cool and cold, with intermittent spells of bloody freezing, we were both suffering from a case of confused heat exhaustion.

We wandered into town in the hope of finding a bar in which to get some cold drinks, but they all appeared to be closed. However, we found the Inter-Hotel du Chateau with its tables and chairs placed wonderfully under a welcoming canopy. We both ordered coffee and long iced lemonades. While we re-hydrated we considered, following such a frustratingly heated day, whether it would be prudent to enquire if we could book a room for the night in the hotel, rather than camp. It didn't take much considering and luckily they had a room for us with…….air conditioning and even provided a separate building in which I could secure Pablo, fantastic!

We hot tailed it back to Camping de Gouarec, took down the tent and was back at the hotel in about 3 hours. What a relief it was to peel my sweat encrusted cycle gear from my overheated body, have a much needed cool shower and relax with the room air conditioning set to maximum chill.

Without the need to cook our evening meal we strolled into town and found a table in Le Vesuve, a small independent pizzeria. While eating we detected other northern English voices, and they appeared to be voicing a decision of some kind. The voices belonged to Barry and Joan from Bolton, and they did indeed have a decision to make, a rather important and life-changing one. On hearing our Yorkshire twang, they came over for a natter. It turned out that Barry and Joan were taking part in the Channel 4 TV program, 'A Place in the Sun: Home or Away'. Having completed just about all of the filming in Lancashire and Brittany, they had taken the opportunity to go out for an evening meal while they decided whether to buy either at home, away, or whether to buy at all. As we swapped our tales about France over coffees, we not only found out that Barry and Joan, the TV crew, including the famed presenter Jonnie Irwin, were staying at the same hotel as us, we also discovered the outcome of Barry and Joan's decision. However, as the Home or Away TV programs are often repeated, and you may be a fan and enjoy the suspense, I won't spoil your fun by letting on. I'll just ask the question, given the choice of buying a two-up-two-down in Lythm St Anne's near Blackpool, or a detached 4 bedroom in southern Brittany, both houses for the same amount of money, which one would you go for?

Back at the hotel, just before I crashed out for the night, I'm sure I heard a clumping on the stairway and the dulcet tones of Mr Irwin talking, or could it have been someone nearby so bored they were watching British TV re-runs?

I suppose I could have asked Jonnie over breakfast, but he seemed confused enough that morning. He'd been speaking with Barry and Joan and they must have been telling him about my trip down to Spain. However he'd somehow got it into his head that I was attempting it on a horse, this was despite having seen me dressed in my cycling gear and packing Pablo for the day. Who knows, maybe it could have been down to all the pressure of having to appear before the cameras again on what was obviously going to be another scorcher. He nevertheless wished me all the best and informed me he thought I was doing it for a fantastically worthy charity. It occurred to me much later in the day I should have tried to tap Channel 4 for a donation, but not to worry, as I write donations are still trickling in, there could still be time.

Having made use of the hotel's secure Wi-Fi, I discovered I'd already more than doubled my target for the charity, with many people donating via my JustGiving site and selecting to use the Gift Aid option. This naturally benefited Yorkshire Cancer Research, but I asked myself was it totally fair for the poor old British taxpayer? If someone chooses to use Gift Aid an extra 25% is added to their donation at no cost to themselves, instead this money is paid by the government. Which in real terms means by the taxpayer, therefore by you and me. With the economy in such a dire state of destitution having readily relined the pockets of those very needy bankers (and although it was tempting, I refrained from using the letter 'w' at the beginning of the word bankers) resulting in many worthy causes loosing funding, I hated to think I was making the situation worse by asking for Gift Aids. It was horrible to contemplate, because someone had been kind enough to donate to Yorkshire Cancer Research and opted for Gift Aid, come freezing December, some poor little mites were going to have to sit chilled to their tiny bones in an unheated temporary built classroom. Or God forbid, the old chap, who because there was no funding for a local bus service, had limped the two miles down to his local library, persevered reading all but the last 10 pages of War and Peace, only to be informed that the library had sold the book that very morning to an internet book collector, who just happened to represent a city banker, to pay for the children's section to keep its five, 1972, I spy books in stock.

After leaving Fenella at the hotel chatting with Barry and Joan and the TV guys, re-joining the towpath to begin La Vélodyssée Section 3 (111.1km), I reflected that sometimes it seems all you do is wrong, by trying to do what is right. That is of course, if you're not a high flying city investor who constantly petitions in Westminster for tax deductions to ensure the central heating is always available in your country estate stables, and your motor cruiser is always fuelled just in case you need to pop down to Monaco for the odd party or two.

Thinking about boats, as I pootled along a thought struck me which perhaps should have registered in my brain much sooner. I'd followed the Nantes/Brest canal for about 90km, and up to that point I hadn't seen a single boat, dingy, canoe or any other type of water-going craft whatsoever. For such a rich vein of water borne capability, I found this fact to be puzzling to say the least. Back in Britain it seemed every single canal, large or small, was bustling with just about every sort of vessel it was possible to launch. Were the French allergic to inland waterways I wondered? Or was it because with the glory days of canals being the primary route for transporting cargo around the country long gone, as a people, didn't the French possess that very British precondition to be on, in, or at the very least to be near water of some sort or other?

The answer is more complicated. Brittany began the organised development of its waterways as far back as 1538, and the Nantes/Brest Canal was officially opened in 1858, following a 47 year construction. At 360km long and with 218 locks along its way the canal was France's most ambitious waterway project. But it ended as a navigational route in 1920 when a section was submerged by the Guerlédan Dam west of Pontivy, and in 1957 the entire waterway west of Guerlédan was closed. The consequential loss of commercial traffic, usually 26m long barges carrying up to 140 tonnes, meant the canal began to silt up reducing some sections between locks to just 0.90m in depth, providing the answer as to why I wasn't sharing my travels with waterborne traffic of any kind. But past the town of Rohan, drawing near the beautiful town of Josselin all that was about to change.

The heat was continuing to build as I approached Josselin, but as I rounded a sweeping bend the first sight of the town made me forget my sun drenched blues as I gazed towards the stunning vista before me. Extensively considered to be one of the most impressive châteaux in the whole of Brittany, Château du Josselin dominates the town and provides a magnificent visual to anyone approaching by road, canal, or as in my case, towpath.

Legend has it that the town developed after a small chapel was built on the site where, in 808AD, a labourer discovered a wooden statue covered by brambles, and on clearing the brambles the sight of his blind daughter miraculously returned. As the town grew a château was built early in the 11th century, but was completely destroyed by King Henry II of England, with rebuilding beginning in 1173.

Further notoriety grew around the town when in 1351, during the Hundred Years War, in an attempt to try and wind-up what had become a military stalemate, two groups of approximately 30 English knights, under the leadership of Robert Bramborough, the English captain of the Ploërmrel, and Franco-Breton knights, commanded by Jean de Beaumanoir, captain of Josselin, staged an arranged combat at a spot halfway between the Château de Josselin and Ploërmel. The Franco-Breton knights claimed the day killing a number of English knights and capturing the remainder of the English force, including their leader Bramborough. The episode famously became known as the Combat of Thirty.

Further damage occurred to the château in 1629, when Cardinal Richelieu, of The Three Musketeers fame, ordered its partial demolishment. The château fell into almost total dereliction during the 17th and 18th centuries. Until in 1835 the Duke of Rohan began a series of restorations, and today, still under the Rohan's ownership it remains one of just a few châteaux still owned by an old ruling family. Who no doubt also owned one, if not a few, of the many splendid launches bobbing about under the impressive bearing of the château.

It seemed a good place for me to stop for lunch. Finding a shady spot on the lock adjacent to the château I rested my heat-weary bones, laying stretched out on the verdant freshly mowed grass, breathing in the heady aroma of Ammi (Queen Anne's lace), Chrysanthemum, Eucharis (Amazon Lily), and Lily of the Valley (Convallaria). Making it sound as if I know my blooms, which is far from the truth, to me if it's red it's a rose, if it's white it's a daisy, if it's yellow it's a daffodil, and if it's any other colour then I'm horticulturally baffled. It's fair to say I'm no gardener. I have a passing relationship with my garden; I pass through it to get my bike from the shed. However, I was pastorally savvy enough to photograph the small information board detailing the flowers planted, and then later search Google for their bracketed sub-names. While I was in a photographic mood I also took a few snaps of the château and surrounding area for Fenella to view later, as her driving route on the N24 bypassed Josselin.

It was only a short 15km ride to Le Roc, where we'd booked a campsite for the night. Cycling along accompanied by the rock-and roll, the splutter and the pop-pop of accompanying craft, as opposed to the loneliness of constantly viewing my wavering shadowy profile and having to listen to the monotonous swish of Pablo's tyres, I felt heaps more serene. After about 3 days of almost surreal watery solitude, the canal had at last sprung into vibrant life.

It seemed the towpath had sprung into life too, a slithery type of life. I know this because for the first time in all my days of cycling I ran over a snake, or I should say, nearly ran over a snake. It must have been contentedly sunning itself on the path when it sensed me trundling along and just before my front wheel hit it tried to slither away. Unfortunately, at the very second it tried to move I spotted it and swerved to miss, only to swerve in the same direction it was moving, the result being that for a short while the poor thing became entangled in the spokes of my front wheel. Not knowing what type of snake it was, or knowing if it was one of the three types of venomous snakes found in France, I could only stare at it in a sort of bemused wonderment. As our eyes locked it also looked rather surprised and I suspect more than a little angry at its predicament before it speedily disentangled itself and slithered into the undergrowth along the side of the towpath. From later research I discovered it was probably a Western Whip Snake (Coluber Viridiflavus), a non-venomous sun-loving snake that is a 'sit and wait' predator, feeding on lizards and small birds and mammals by wrapping itself around its prey and suffocating it. I guess it must have been in sit and wait mode as I came along, but thankfully it didn't try and suffocate Pablo's front tyre, nevertheless measuring-in at about 70cm in length I'd bet good money if it had been hungry enough it would have given it a good go.

It was about 3pm when I met Fenella at Domaine-du-Roc Camping. Meaning an early finish to the day for me. Also, for a change to our routine to date, plenty of time for us to get the tent set-up, put our feet up for an afternoon doze, followed by a long cool swim in the outdoor pool, and to have a couple of cold beers before we ventured out for a bite to eat. However, the last bit proved to be somewhat tricky.

On enquiring at the campsite reception, Madam Helene the campsite owner, informed us that in and around Le Roc it was traditional that from Friday lunchtime until Saturday morning all the local businesses close up for that period, including the eateries. However, she informed us the Hotel de la Gare may still remain open, and if so Madam Clémence would, 'look after us', which sounded a little worrying to me.

It was only a short stroll along the towpath and over the bridge to the Hotel, which on first site looked to be on its way to tumbling down, with nowhere else to choose from, with a forced breath of anticipation we ventured inside. With décor that looked like it had last seen a lick of paint a couple of decades sometime before Charles de

Gaulle first took up his presidency, the whole of the front part of the Hotel was laid out with long trestle tables set for dinner, with each table set for about twenty people. It was totally deserted. I was ready to scarper, but before I had a chance to run an elderly lady, who must have been well into her eighties came shakily out of a doorway and waved us greetings. This, we presumed, must be the famed Madam Clémence.

I felt trapped, but much braver than me, Fenella asked if she was open for food. Giving a brief nod, she grabbed two sets of cutlery from one of the trestle tables, laid them down on an unset table nearer the doorway she had appeared from, and indicated we should sit there. She then pointed to a menu scribbled on a blackboard which was propped on a disused table, and wandered back through the doorway. The menu indicated a set meal of; liver paté for the first course, a choice of pork or steak with veg for the main and either cheese and biscuits or Tarte au lait caillé for sweet. After a couple of minutes she returned with a couple of plates and glasses and without a word of enquiry plonked a 1.5 litre bottle of red wine down for us to share, she then wandered back through her doorway to return with a large plate of crusty home baked bread and a homemade dish of paté which was just about the size of a small bathtub. It was bloody gorgeous, and without doubt the best paté I've ever tasted. While we were eating she came and pointed at the menu in an enquiry of which main we wanted, Fenella chose the pork and I went for the steak. Finished eating what we thought was a greedy amount of paté, popping her head through the doorway our silent host seemed surprised we hadn't eaten it all and indicated with her hands we should help ourselves to more. Already feeling stuffed, our next courses were put before us, half a medium-sized pig for Fenella and one side of a cow for me, both with tinned peas and carrots. Fenella's pork was cooked to perfection, tender with a trim of crispy crackling, I too prefer my meat on the well done side. However, I wasn't going to show myself up, and I gamely worked my way through my steak, which may or may not have experienced some form of heat, although I'm certain that would have been in the way of sunshine and when it was last able to stand on its own four legs and chew grass. It was still damned good though. Fenella finished her meal with a selection of cheese and biscuits and I tried the Tarte au lait caillé, which was very enjoyable and turned out to be rather like a deep sided curd tart. The whole bill came to 27 euros, just over 23 quid for two home cooked three course meals and 1.5 litres of red wine. Talk about never judging a book by its cover. Unbelievably fantastic! Thanks Madam Clémence.

Back at the campsite our neighbour had returned to his small Eriba caravan and in broken English, which was still far better than our pigeon French, told us how much he treasured wandering the canal, exploring the area around Le Roc and in particular spending his weekends relaxing at Domaine-du-Roc Camping. I had to agree, it was the best campsite we'd found so far. It enjoyed a tremendous location right alongside the canal, it held all the amenities a camper/caravanner, including a section of immaculate 1960's caravans which were let-out to holidaymakers wanting that nostalgic experience, and it presented a friendly welcoming atmosphere to all.

Sitting in the still of the Brittany countryside, with the night creeping in, after such a pleasing day it seemed it would have been fitting to slip on a Peter Sarstedt track, and like his lost love, sip on Napoleon brandy without getting our lips wet. But we didn't have any 60's greatest hits compilations and I've never been able to drink without getting my lips wet, at least not without a straw. So instead we played The Beatles had a mug or two of Yorkshire tea and got our lips soaked.

I didn't mention my incident with the snake to Fenella until we were tucked in our sleeping bags and I'm sure in the darkness of the tent the slithering noise I heard wasn't another snake, rather I suspect it was Fenella slipping to the bottom of her sleeping bag and firmly folding over the top just in case.

Château de Josselin

Leaving Le Roc for another day
cycling the Brest/Nantes Canal

It was obvious the following morning that it was going to be even hotter. According to the car dashboard readout at 08.30 the temperature was already 34^{0}C, and by the look of it without a cloud on the French side of the Alps. Our friendly neighbour had already left for the day and most of the nostalgic caravaner's were breakfasting alfresco. We did the same, and after making sure I was well sun-creamed up and Pablo was loaded to the gunnels with energy snacks and drinkable liquids I hit the towpath towards Redon to complete my journey through Brittany.

That particular stretch of towpath between Le Roc and Redon was perhaps the best I'd cycled to date, wonderfully level and seemingly without a blemish to its surface. Even where large oak trees closely bordered the track, during the whole distance of around 50km of cycling I didn't come across a single tree root breaking the trail surface. Wonderful, given that even on the best tarmacked British trails if anything larger than a 3ft wild privet acts as a border the whole of the track surface becomes a criss-crossed maze of lumpy bulges and bumps, making for a dreadfully uncomfortable ride. It appeared to me as I whooshed along that the French authorities really consider and appreciate their cyclists and are prepared to spend money to care for their welfare. Whereas in contrast, the British authorities are keen to vocalise about supporting cycling and cyclists, particularly during election times. But when it comes down to spending hard cash on their behalf that becomes a different story, they would rather waste taxpayers money on large rail projects, such as HS2, and making the motorways a great deal more dangerous by turning the hard shoulders into extra carriageways to get more 40 ton juggernauts along them. Apart from a few decent inner city and out of town cycle ways, little real consideration is given to the British cyclist's safety.

As I approached Redon, changing gears to climb from the trail into town, an alarming crunching sound came from Pablo's rear gear block and my back wheel locked completely nearly throwing me headfirst into the canal. Fearing the worst, imagining broken gearing, twisted spokes and a buckled rear wheel, with trepidation I dismounted to investigate. What I found surprised me. Somehow a long bootlace had become completely and excruciatingly entangled in Pablo's rear gear meshing. At first I couldn't figure it out, where had it come from? Then I realised, it was the lace I'd been using as an extra fastening for my rear bag. I couldn't have tied it properly when I'd last been in my bag hunting for my camera, it must have slipped to become snagged in Pablo's rear mech. I wondered how the hell I could get it out, I thought about cutting it into small pieces, but I didn't have any scissors, or even a penknife. Finding a length that was not so tightly snared, I twisted it around two fingers and simply yanked with all my might. Initially nothing happened, except the lace began to cut deeply into my fingers. However, thankfully Pablo's gearing slowly began to reverse, his rear wheel spun backwards and the lace slipped free. Phew! I'm not the most understanding of modern indexed derailleur systems and I wasn't sure what would have happened if it hadn't come free.

My first impressions of Redon was its similarity to Morlaix, an inland town built around a large central harbour. With a rich heritage, water is at the heart of Redon, it is where the Nantes/Brest canal crosses the River Vilaine via a double lock system. In the 18th century Redon was the primary French port dealing in the salt trade and the original salt barns and warehouses can still be found shouldering the waterside today. With construction beginning in the 9th century, Redon's Saint Sauveur Abbey is one of the largest in Brittany and still holds documents detailing the early life of the Abbey.

Nevertheless, for all its cultural history and the bustling beauty of its modern-day attractions, as well as Redon being the final location of my journey through Brittany, the other aspects of the town that concerned me were just how bloody hot it was, and where I could buy a cold drink and something sweet to eat. Opposite the port I appreciatively spied a boulangerie with its door's still thrown open for custom. Phoning Fenella, who was conveniently driving the outskirts of town, I rushed inside before the staff could lock their doors for their mid-day break, as had happened when I'd become lost in Cleguérec. I bought four cans of iced cola and two large deliciously looking tranche de vanilla's. On Fenella's arrival we sat in the shade of the boulangeriés overhanging canopy and supped down the canned coolness, munched our sugary confections, and I reflected on my trip through Brittany.

I thought overall it had been a success. Initially I'd located La Vélodyssée much easier than I had imagined. Admittedly, I'd buggered Pablo's pedal system up, and confirmed to Fenella my Le Routard booklet was still safe and sound, I'd had a snake join me for company and I'd been a little lost and a little found. We'd discovered good and not-so good campsites, plus a welcoming hotel complete with TV crew and we'd met some fantastic folk. The heat had been unexpectedly draining, yet, via old railway routes, a seemingly endless canal towpath, which included a number of confusing diversions, I'd somehow managed to end up in the right place, and to boot, slightly quicker than I thought possible.

As for Brittany itself, with my cycle trip being my first visit to the region, I found it to be stunningly beautiful, charming and extremely picturesque. I also thought it to be pleasantly old fashioned, in a way that happily harped back to how I fondly remember South Yorkshire to be in the early to mid-1960's, very jigsaw-box. Which perhaps gave the reason as to why so many 60's songs had been popping in my head, and why I'd been using them to associate the happenings of my trip up to that juncture. I knew I must return to Brittany sometime, and still without giving too much away, I hoped Barry and Joan will enjoy living in the area.

Part 3

Propelling Pays de la Loire – Ha Ha Said The Clown (Manfred Mann)

With Redon being the end of La Vélodyssée Section 3 it wasn't the close of my day's cycling. Back on the towpath to begin La Vélodyssée Section 4 (103.8km), shortly after leaving the town it did however appear that it was the end of the fantastic quality of the track. But it wasn't because of any tree rooting, surface weathering, or poor workmanship, it was as if someone had been out with a shovel randomly digging deep holes at unevenly spaced intervals. Why, I couldn't hazard a guess, maybe someone had a grudge against cyclists and thought their sporadic excavations would upset and disrupt the smoothness of the cycling community of Redon and similarly any passing tourists like myself.

It didn't work, not that I've ever been smooth in any way, more dishevelled and haggardly unkempt. No, I was less bothered about the surface and more concerned about the positioning of the track. It had considerably narrowed to closely hug the main railway line at a height that put my head perfectly on a level with the speeding express train's wheelbases. Which with every passing train made me instinctively duck my head and veer sideways. A manoeuvre that was dangerous to say the least as the towpath had risen a good 20ft above the canal with only a short unsubstantial wire fence protecting me from a fall into what for the first time had become a grimy stagnant looking lump of water. It all made for a wobbly, gnarly, and has to be said, 'English trail' ride towards La Grulais, where La Vélodyssée once again returned to being French and thus, a premier quality cycleway and the canal into a clear healthy waterway.

By 4pm I'd had enough, the heat was making it dangerously uncomfortable to cycle. I was beginning to feel dizzy and nauseous and knew that if I didn't stop for the day I could have well collapsed in an untidy heap of broiled old fool. I met Fenella at Guenrouët where we managed to buy ice lollies before the drive back to Domaine-du-Roc Camping, where we'd thoughtfully decided to leave the tent for another night.

A few more cyclists had arrived during the day, including a group of four young lads with creaky old bikes and a homemade cycle trailer that looked as if it had been made from a plastic waste recycle box. While still out for a good time, they were happy, well behaved, well-mannered pleasant young lads, and they'd obviously cycled there, good for them I thought.

Sipping cool beer, cooking our evening meal of ravioli and watching the lads cook their evening meal on a small disposable barbeque, I reflected how fortunate I was in comparison. They were cycling on what could be classed as old crocks, while I had a new purpose built lightweight touring bike. They had a selection of diminutive shabby one-man tents, with not even enough tent pegs to go around. I was going to sleep in a roomy, inflatable shelter, which in contrast was of pavilion sized proportions. They'd carried all their gear themselves in a home-produced wonky-wheeled trailer, while I had Fenella and her Volvo to carry my stuff around. However, a couple of things they did have as advantages over me were, 1) cycling as a group. Meaning when one of them was drained and feeling down, he'd have the others to put a metaphorical arm around him to help get him through the testing time. I was cycling solo, and although I could meet with Fenella occasionally, when I was riding, with tens of kilometres between one stop and another, when I hit a low ebb, the only person who could coax me out of it was myself. 2) Each one of the lads had at least 40 years on me, and in spite of feeling Ok fitness wise up to that point, I still wouldn't have minded offloading a good 30 years or so, not to mention swapping a headful of grey hairs for my youthful dark brown mop.

So as the day drew towards another balmy night, I decided I'd better remain as age intended. I consoled myself with the thought that whatever advantages and disadvantages I and the young lads had between us, that particular night we'd all ended up in the same place, we all appeared to be fit and well, and the following day, with luck, we'd all again be heading along our chosen paths of destination.

The sun had us crawling from our tent before 7am. We couldn't believe it was obviously going to be even warmer than the previous day. Even at that time of the morning the heat was so intense I got the feeling that the sun had been enthusiastically counting the seconds awaiting our awakening, although the forecast was for electrical storms towards evening. The heat had awoken most other folk too. The tented estate was alive with the sights and smells of early morning campsite operations; the stretching of sleep numbed limbs, bodies venting unwanted gaseous pressurisations, hurried toilet block manoeuvres, teeth being scrubbed, kettles boiling, egg shells breaking, bacon frying. It all bypassed the four lads, they still dozed on in contented teenager oblivion.

Absolutions completed, breakfasted, decamped, car packed, maps organised, body protection on in the forms of chamois cream, factor 50 and anti-midge spray, I was back on the bike before 0830. I figured to get most of the kilometres under my belt before 2pm.

Still cycling the Brest/Nantes towpath I began to notice changes in the surrounding landscape. Gone were the rather claustrophobic borders of barbarous entangled hedgerows, statuesque deciduous and swaying conifers, replaced by open fields of mature wheat crops, ram-rod rows of snap beans and sprouting corn-on-the cob.

Between Bain and Nort-sur-Erdre I saw my first angler too. Which I thought odd. Not that he was odd in any way. Odd in the fact that if I'd been cycling a towpath for days upon days back in Britain, I'd have passed hundreds of maggot danglers decorating the side of the canal with their array of rods, poles, nets, bait boxes, float and hook chests, seats, trailers and four-season shelters not to mention their camouflaged clothing that would look more suitable on a battlefield than on a peaceful canal side.

Fishing is never a sport (I use the term 'sport' in a loose sense) that I could get into, although once when much younger, when I had far less body and much more hair, I gave it a try. My late and sorely missed brother-in-law Gerald was a skilled and dedicated angler and having arranged that I purchase all the tackle I would need from a mate of his, he took me off to the River Torn, in what was then South Humberside, for my induction into the world of freshwater fishing. As the balmy late May afternoon progressed, 20 yards from where I plonked myself, Gerald managed to net fish after fish after bloody fish. I caught zilch. 'You're much too animated', he instructed, 'stop hutching and moving about, sit still, think about the river, think about what you're doing and you'll feel the water communicate with you'.

I became a statue of concentration. Gerald caught on and on, yet for me, nothing, not even a twitch on my rod. I sat without moving the proverbial muscle, hardly even daring to blink an eye, and eventually just as Gerald predicted, the Torn and I became one. Locked in my silent static pose a large thrush landed on my head making me bound-up in shock, and on the loose banking, with rod and nets flying in all directions, I raucously fell headlong into the river. My fishing days were over, and guess my downer about fishing isn't because of the pastime itself, no, it's because I was so bloody useless at it. I don't miss fishing, but I do miss Gerald.

Another sight on that stretch of towpath that reminded me of my younger days was that of a nun, palms upwards in deep prayer. But this one was out of luck, there were no small children about to beat up. I say that from having been taught by nuns from the age of 7, first in a convent and then through a series of strict Catholic schools up to the age of 16, when I at last managed to break free from their sadistic rituals of making kids feel that on some days not even God liked them. My mate Lawrence, who you've already been introduced to and my friend Linda also came along on that journey as we moved from school to school, always in the same class, always in the same set, always together in the vicinity of those monochrome tormentors. I often wonder what they think when they see a nun, do they feel the same aversions about them as me? Having shared the same and sometimes physically persecuted experiences, my guess is they do.

I wondered watching the nun talking silently to God, whether she was still in touch with the living, was she aware of the day? Was she aware of the real? I knew I was, and I knew just how unpleasant the heat of the real was making me feel. Pablo seemed to weigh a ton, it was as if the flat had become a steep gradient, each pedal stroke was physically more difficult than the last. I began to cycle in a trance-like state of lethargy. No matter how much liquid I poured into myself with each kilometre I was becoming increasingly more dehydrated, no matter how many energy jellies I scoffed my weariness intensified. To use the cyclists term of becoming completely knackered, I'd bonked.

Also, the day itself had a persecuting air about it, towards Nantes and the south west the sky looked so threateningly heavy it appeared as if it was about to collapse earthwards. The expression that kept popping to mind was that of the Dads Army character, Private Frazer, played by the great actor John Laurie, 'we're all doomed, doomed I say!'. Yes, the day had a certain doom about it, a very real doom. I began to wonder if Mrs Nun knew something I didn't, was her God about to wreak havoc on humanity, or me for my dislike of her kind, or was it about to piss it down before I reached the city?

I met Fenella at Le Pont du Plessis, 30km north of Nantes. As we sat in a shaded sandy area adjacent to the towpath, while I drank and drank, with the sky looking so menacing, not thinking it wise to camp we researched possible hotels for the night. It was in this part of France I reverted to what some folk may describe as a typical outmoded northern English bloke on his hols. I draped a large paisley patterned neckerchief over my head which I regularly dowsed with liberal quantities of cold water, sighing with pained pleasure as the cooling balm in blissful slow-motion dribbled down my overheated torso. For all the world it looked like I was the archetypal 1960's day-tripper, sat on Blackpool beach staring nonsensically at the parading donkeys, modelling a poorly knotted hankie perched on my head. I know this because Fenella 'kindly' took a photo of me, which for the unfortunate viewing public may see the light of day someday.

We decided upon the Westotel at La Chaplle-sur-Erdre. Constructed in shimmering steel and glass, under the deepening skies it all looked very classy, with glittering crystal chandeliers and life-sized Romanesque statues gracing the vast marbled reception area. I must also award five stars to the Madame behind the reception desk. She didn't bat an eyelid as I trooped rather damply across the spotless marbling in my salt crusted sweat-stained bright orange cycling top, slightly askew dusty padded shorts, gaily sporting a sodden square of decorative cotton on my head. Although as Fenella arranged a double room for the night, this elegantly attired professional couldn't resist giving me a cursory look up and down to politely ask Fenella if she would prefer a room with a bath.

No sooner had we found our room, opened the sliding doors to the balcony when the sky exploded. Fork and sheet lightening illuminated the backdrop of Nantes, torrential rain bounced off the parched landscape in a hissing treble snare, while rolling thunder added the required bass to the discordant opus. All that was missing was the immaculate weeping of David Gilmour's Fender Stratocaster to complete this Pink Floyd(ish) introduction to our evening. It was a good decision not to camp.

As the storm intensified circling the Loire, and Fenella investigating what the hotel had to offer in the way of food, I took the receptionists hint and soaked my accumulated grime away in a deep warm bath, the first I'd had since starting my La Vélodyssée. I was happily dozing in luxurious comfort when a huge flash of lightening seemed to strike the hotel exactly outside our room and all the power tripped. There I was, just like in a survival movie, up to my neck in water, alone, in the midst of a roaring storm. I knew I must not panic, I knew with fortitude and inner steadfastness I would endure my predicament. I'd seen many a film in which the survivor steels themselves with the mantra, 'I must stay alert, I can't let myself fall asleep', my very survival now depends on my resolve to keep awake'. The storm had drifted away and Fenella was reading on the balcony when I woke-up an hour or so later. I may not have demonstrated my true survival instincts, but at least I was a lot more spick-and-span than over the previous few days, and like numerous fictional survivors before me, I was more than ready for some grub.

We ate in the hotel, both having the Plate du Jour of Crab Paté, Beef Bourguignon and Tarte aux Pommes. Before sleep we retired to our balcony to share a bottle of red and listen to the booming Pink Floyd tour of the Loire Valley as it spectacularly drifted inland. Because up to that point I'd cycled 7 days consecutively, we discussed the possibility of spending the next day in La

Chaplle-sur-Erdre, allowing me a day's rest from the bike. Fenella was all for it, but knowing my next day of cycling would mean traversing Nantes, not a part of the ride I was looking forward to, I didn't fancy putting it off any longer than necessary and decided I would prefer to get it over and done with the following day.

Pablo having a well-deserved
rest outside our tent

Hot and bothered at Le Pont du Plessis
waiting for the rain to come

I find it can sometimes be frustrating navigating through a large unfamiliar city by bicycle, Nantes didn't prove to be the exception. But before I found myself dazed and confused in the perplexing boulevards of one of France's largest cities I had to bid my farewells to the Brest/Nantes Canal.

From Le Pont du Plessis, cycling the last few kilometres of the towpath I found the previous night's storm had created advantages and disadvantages. It was certainly cooler than the preceding days had been, with the temperature dropping back into the high twenties, making it much easier to breath. The resulting moisture had made the canal's wildlife make appearances. Enormous jet-black undulating masses appeared and disappeared on the canal surface, these were formed by hundreds of tiny fish congregating in one place and then suddenly diving and darting to re-form heaving shoals a few metres away. Stunning Crescent Bluet dragonfly's skimmed along the surface, at times closely pacing me at head height. Palmate Newts stared boggled-eyed at my passage and dappled Sand Lizards scuttled away from my spinning wheels; thankfully though, I didn't spot anymore basking snakes. With that section of the towpath being sand based, as my tyres began to cut into the rain softened surface I had to balance with great care to ensure I didn't take a tumble, and sloppy gritty debris began to pebble Pablo's framing and gear train. It all made for a slushy goodbye to La Vélodyssée Section 4 and the exquisite towpath I'd cycled for almost 250km.

Beginning La Vélodyssée Section 5 (96km), before entering Nantes, adjacent to the River L'Erdre, using a combination of traffic-free bridleways I passed through a number of hamlet's including La Grande Bodinière, La Guillonnière and La Turbalière, all being picture perfect in their own jigsaw box kind of way. Leaving La Turbalière I met my second pair of cycling Brits since the couple I'd passed who were in the midst of a disagreement, not including Andy and Elvis who weren't in the process of cycling when we met and chatted. I realised they were Brits when the lead cyclist came barrelling downhill towards me on the wrong side of the bridleway on an old 1980's Raleigh Sprint and veering to just miss me, looking over his shoulder instead of where he was going and yelling for all his worth, 'Linda, Linda! Watch out, bike, bike, a bike!'

I met Linda at the crest of the hill riding perfectly calmly and in control and on the correct side of the track. Who presumably thinking I was French, said, 'Je suis désolé monsieur, il est toujours comme ça quand il monte à vélo'.

Covering an area of around 70 square km, Nantes, the sixth largest city in France with an urban population of 600,000 inhabitants, a student population of 40,000 and an endless number of summer visitors came as a bit of a shock to the system given that I'd been mainly cycling through villages and hamlets with a population in the 10's to the 100's at the most. With an extended history as an industrial and commercial centre and major French Port, Nantes advertises itself as being, 'the nicest city in

France, rich, lively, innovative and France's second largest city in terms of growth'. It is home to the restored medieval Château des Ducs de Bretagne, where the Dukes of Brittany once lived. The castle is now a local history museum with multimedia exhibits, as well as a walkway on the top of its fortified ramparts.

La Vélodyssée took me into the heart of the city via the sprawling University de Nantes, at first the route signage was fine but on entering the city centre my problems began. Following the Rue de l'Eveché, to the rear of La Cathédrale Saint-Pierre-et-Saint-Paul, I lost La Vélodyssée signs completely. Hunting for signs as I cycled up and down Rue Henry IV, I found myself being shadowed by an annoying clown on a unicycle, who from his manic giggling appeared to revel in the fact that I was obviously lost. Spending the last 20 years working in education this naturally was not the first time I've been in the close vicinity of clowns, although very few were on unicycles, wearing an Andy-Pandy suit and a huge red nose. Most of the clowns I came across tended to walk with an air of self-appointed arrogance, wore power suits and a badge identifying them to be either Senior Management or an Ofsted Inspector. They were just as foolishly annoying.

No matter how hard I searched I couldn't locate a sign to get me out of the city centre. Still stalked by the laughing clown, I was, however, beginning to appreciate just what a rich and innovative city Nantes was developing into. Close to the cathedral, all bumping into one another, I found a bank, a gay and lesbian sex boutique, an opticians and a McDonalds. So without moving location it was possible to: 1) draw some cash, 2), visit the boutique, 3), buy some specs, nip back into the boutique to check some finer details, 4) get your energy back with a burger or two, 5) I'll not detail number five as this is not a violent book, 6) cross the street to repent. Although in this day and age I think clown-throttling should be classed as morally acceptable and therefore repentance not strictly necessary. All of which didn't help me at all in my quest for an escape from the city.

Never spotting a La Vélodyssée sign I found the next best thing, a large street plan board, from which I figured the best way to leave the city, and get to the south side of the Loire, was to do so by cycling on and off the Ile De Nantes. At last managing to free myself from the laughing clown, I achieved this by following a tram heading towards the Ile, then used the Pont Georges Clemenceau Bridge to navigate myself onto the south bank.

I'd agreed to meet Fenella at Le Pellerin, but I couldn't see a cycle route signed, the only choice I could find were routes leading towards Pont Saint-Martin or Verton, neither of which were on my mapping. Abandoning my map and instead keeping the Loire towards my right I followed the roadways through the towns of Rezé, Bouguenais, La Montagne, and St-Jean-de Boiseau. Which when written sounds so simple, but in reality involved many a dead end, looping back on myself and visiting a number of featureless residential and shopping areas. In one of which, outside an indoor market in Bouguenais, hearing a young Mademoiselle speaking English and asking her if I was correctly heading towards Le Pellerin, she in turn asked me firstly, why I wanted to go there, 'as it was boring and no good to visit'. Secondly she informed me, 'I'd be much better off visiting Cholet'. Which given the fact I was on a bike, and whether a nice place or not, Cholet was 60k in the wrong direction, meaning unfortunately her advice didn't prove to be the most helpful.

Following a few more wrong turns and unintended stopovers towards 5pm I at last succeeded in reacquainting myself with La Vélodyssée at La Noë and began my run-in to Le Pellerin. This in itself proved to be frustrating as the route was formed from a series of zigzagging switchbacks lasting around 18k which swung sharply downhill, only to shortly about turn and go steeply back uphill. In terms of distance covered it felt as if I'd been cycling on the spot.

I made it to Le Pellerin and met with Fenella at 6.15pm, making for a long and challenging day of riding. I'd rode for over 7 hrs and covered only about 50km. Also, after all that effort I discovered that the Mademoiselle I'd spoken with in Bouguenais had proved herself to be spot on with her critique of Le Pellerin. In truth, her description of the place as being 'boring' seemed to be an understatement. From our findings Le Pellerin materialised to be no more than a large car park serving a ferry crossing from the north bank, with one shabby looking hotel which wouldn't look out of place in an early François Truffaut movie and a solitary cheerless bar full of sullen looking patrons. From its position alongside the muddied waters of the Loire it was of interest to note that Le Pellerin was twinned with the River Humber town of North Ferriby, which if you've ever had the pleasure of visiting perhaps says a lot.

On the other hand, we found an interesting place to stay for the night, Les Mandalas, Chambres d'hôtes, a small complex of gites, seemingly run on the same principle as Southfork from the TV series Dallas. There was mini Pam Ewing to greet us at the electronic gates and talkatively show us her estate. All the while mini Bobby remained out of sight, presumably still asleep and having nightmares about the terrible possibility that Emmanuel Macron was the President of France, Donald Trump had bizarrely become President of the USA, Theresa May was still the Prime Minster of Great Britain, who as a nation had inexplicably voted to abandon his beloved E.U. Thankfully he didn't awaken during our stay forcing us to explain to him it really wasn't all of our doing, other folk had been involved too.

We ate in Pornic, my destination for the preceding day and then returned to Southfork to have a couple of cold beers before retiring for the night. About 3am I was awoken by a strange clomping. Turning on the light I found a grasshopper, who from the size and noise he was making, must have been directly related to Skippy the Bush Kangaroo. Opening the bathroom door there were so many strange night time creatures hopping and bopping around it was like stepping into Jurassic Park.

Fenella used so much insecticide spray she set the fire alarm going! It took us a good 15 minutes to clear the results of her assault up. In the end we just chucked the bodies out of the window. I'm not sure if it was a dodo I lobbed out, it just went along with the peregrine, pelican and the penguin

During breakfast, which to me felt more like a job interview than a morning meal due to the extraordinarily inquisitiveness of Pam, our presiding mini hostess (mini Bobby doubtless still dreaming away), I was surprised to find another pair of cyclists being similarly cross-examined. They and their families must have arrived at Les Mandalas after we'd fallen asleep. They weren't cycling La Vélodyssée, but had brought their bikes to the Loire region to cycle wherever their fancy took them. While I was planning to follow the river to its estuary at Pont de St-Nazaire on the south bank, and then onwards towards Pornic, they planned to cycle southwards in an attempt to circle the Réserve Naturelle de Grand-Lieu, a ride of around 70km.

Back at Le Pellerin I began by cycling the flat unwavering surface alongside the Canal de la Martinière to Paimbœf, which was as easy as it sounds. But from Paimbœf La Vélodyssée used a series of narrow lanes which crisscrossed the busy D77 and once again signage became a problem. On the outskirts of La Herse I was overtaken by a couple of French cyclists, one of which had the complete La Vélodyssée route book in her front basket, unlike me risking the safety of her book by bringing it out into the fresh air. 'Great', I thought, hopefully they would know where they were going, and if they were following La Vélodyssée, if I trailed them at a distance I'd be fine in spite of the lack of signs. This plan worked for about 5km until they pulled off on a grass verge and began to unload picnic gear for an early lunch. I know cyclists are a friendly bunch, but I reckoned I'd be pushing it if I rolled up and joined them with munching their fare, so I tootled past with just a friendly wave, 2km later I was lost.

In the village of La Greix I could hear the traffic on the D77 and having no other alternative I thought I'd better make my way to the road and risk cycling along with the traffic, but then inspiration hit me. It would be nice to say I'd had a fantastic and inventive idea, but to be honest it was bloody obvious, it was something I should have thought of a number of times previously when stuck with lack of signs, use my Garmin Sat Nav. 'You bloody idiot', I cursed; I'd been carrying the thing around for days and had totally forgotten about it. When I'd been lost the previous day and had later complained to Fenella about my mishaps, I presumed she must have thought I'd used my Garmin anyway, because thinking about it, what damn fool wouldn't have?

Hoping for the best I programmed my Garmin for Pornic, via St-Brevin-les-Pins and St Michel-Chef-Chef. I say hoping because the few times I'd used the device, on more than one occasion I must have programmed it incorrectly because as soon as I left my location it had repeatedly routed me back to that point. During one frustrating incident I'd set a route through the town of Runcorn and on to the city of Chester, only to cycle in circles for nearly 2 hours to find myself back where I'd started. This was made more embarrassing because I'd met another cyclist making his way to Chester and I'd persuaded him to follow me. I don't think he was very impressed, but at least he'd seen a few areas of Runcorn that weren't on his itinerary.

So it was not without a little trepidation that I began to follow my Garmin's pictorial mapping directions. My apprehension intensified as I snaked the maze of unnamed lanes edging the village of La Hauté Prinais when I met the couple of cyclists I'd been following earlier, the trouble was they were going in the opposite direction to me. This put me in a dilemma, either trust in my Garmin, or again follow the cyclists. I decided on the Garmin, and despite the couple having La Vélodyssée route book I hoped they weren't actually following the route southwards, because if they were, then I was heading back to Roscoff!

I still had doubts about my decision when my Garmin directed me along a scruffy lane and through the middle of a large traveller's camp. I know political correctness should refrain me from commenting about what a ratty corner of Pays de la Loire this was, and many 'good folk' would argue that I remark about the social deprivation that caused the traveller's to live in such a state. But sod PC, it was bloody unpleasant to cycle through. I had to bump my way over endless trailing electric leads and plastic water pipes, around masses of rotting garbage, reeking mounds of what look like human and animal waste (shit), and pile upon pile of toughened electric cabling, which I've no doubt once belonged to Frances Société Nationale des Chemins de Fer (SNCF) and would later be burnt so the inner steel/copper wiring could be retrieved as bargaining. I was glowered at with obvious malice by anyone who caught my eye, including a tatty pony who gaped at me through a broken window from the inside of a lopsided rundown caravan. PC or not, the folk my sympathy lay with are the locals who have the misfortune of living close to the foetid eyesore, and I can honestly say I was relieved to leave the dump behind me and to get through it safely and in one piece.

Thankfully it wasn't too long before I reached a short section of off-road cycle track hugging the shoreline of the Loire, and I could view the 1,115m long Saint-Nazaire Bridge, which links Saint-Nazaire on the north bank to St-Brevin-les-Pins on the south. With an array of viewpoint seating to choose from, I also reckoned it a worthy place to stop for a rest, a slurp or two from my bidon and to have a munch of my fruit and nut rations.

Still putting faith in my sat nav and despite being several kilometres inland of the Côte de Jade, through St-Michel-Chef-Chef and on to Pornic, I could detect the imposing presence of the Océan Atlantique. Westwards the sky took on a deeper hue of cyan. The air felt fresh, pure, as if scoured of impurities by the oceanic salt, the atmosphere mimicked the connotation of the coast's name, Jade; '.....a sweet, light and nourishing energy that can feel very healing..... a soothing purity.'

Pornic, the close of La Velodyssee Section 5, was an important destination on my trip being the beginning of my run-down of the west coast of France, but for our nights kip we'd booked another night at Les Mandalas and on the drive back we discussed the fact that I still hadn't had a day's rest from cycling, but we were both in agreement that Les Mandalas was not the place for that to happen. In many respects it was an agreeable retreat with a pleasant room, beautiful and spacious landscaped gardens, even a heated swimming pool, yet for all that I didn't feel fully at ease while I was there, and Fenella could sense my disquiet. I had the impression that as guest's part of our duty was to reveal to mini Pam all our thoughts and views upon life, as if she were keeping a little red book about all the folk who visited, in readiness for when Bobby awoke and the day of reckoning began. We decided I would cycle one more day, head for St-Jean-de-Monts and have a rest day at one of our favourite campsites Le Pin Parasol, at La Chapelle-Hermier.

We'd bought cheeses, meats, olives, crusty bread, salad and a local white for our evening meal. After showering and a dip in the pool, we ate outside at the poolside. No one was about. Our hostess was conspicuous by her absence and the other cyclists and their families hadn't returned from their circular sojourn. In spite of my reserves about the place it was delightfully relaxing sitting in the falling darkness, with the chatter of birdlife diminishing to a twilight hush, the distant rumble of the ocean and the mellow snoring emanating from the opened bedroom window of the main house. Sleep on Bobby boy I mused, your day will come.

Before I too fell into the land of nod, giving thanks to my sat nav's reliability and to Fenella's forethought for such an excellent gift, I deemed it wise to give the device a boost in case I needed it during the following days. It was at that moment I discovered that along with my La Vélodyssée route book, it's charging unit and lead were also safe, sound, and nestling on the bookshelf at home. Would I ever learn?

Over breakfast, while attempting to deflect the intensity of mini Pam's re-interrogation, we discovered that the other cyclists hadn't had quiet as successful a day as I'd had on the road. They hadn't got anywhere near the Réserve Naturelle de Grand-Lieu, let-alone circumnavigate it. Within a distance of less than 20km they'd both had punctures, and although they'd had spare inner-tubes, and one spare tyre, both punctures were so severe they needed two tyres. Therefore, they'd had to abandon their ride to go in search of a bike shop. I felt for their bad luck. In the UK the road surfaces are in such a terrible state that cyclists don't expect to get too many miles out of a set of tyres before damage occurs, but in France the roads are pretty decent and it's unusual to have so many punctures in such a short distance. Hopefully, the incidents didn't spoil their holiday and they managed to get some agreeable cycling under their belts without further mishap. As for Pablo, he was doing good. Apart from a liberal coating of dust, and the knackered pedal, which was my fault, all was tiptop. Although on my up-and-coming rest day I recognised as well as a thorough cleaning, I'd have to give him a mechanical once-over.

Located on the Brittany Marches, once a line of fortresses between the Duchy of Brittany and the Kingdom of France, opening out onto the Baie de Bourgneuf, on the northern border of the Vendee, Pornic is more of a region than a single town. In 1973 Pornic 'absorbed' neighbouring Sainte-Marie-sur-Mer and Clion-sur-Mer, whose peoples were called respectively Sanminaritains and Clionnais. These former towns are two sub-divisions of the Pornic known today, which interestingly is twinned with the North Yorkshire town of Scalby, a village not a million miles from my Yorkshire home.

Beginning La Vélodyssée Section 6 (137km), I imagined an easy day in the saddle from Pornic down the coast towards St-Jean-de-Monts, from past experience I knew it to be a flat landscape, and I imagined the routing along the coastline would be simple to follow. Once again my premeditations were to be in error.

Ascending from the pretty harbour, snuggling under the dominance of the Château de Pornic, under downcast cloud broken by intermittent warm sunny spells, at first the cycling was easy going. Meandering along a series of interlocking lanes adjacent to the D97, through the villages of La Joselière, La Boutinardière, crossing the D13 and along a green-lane to Le Pré Tarin and La Rairie, I re-crossed the D13 to meet with Fenella for coffee at the bustling seaside resort of Les Moutiers-en-Retz.

Back on the bike and into the small settlement of Les Sables, my La Vélodyssée signs began to be replaced by the much larger, but sparser located, 'Vélocéan' signs. Strangely following these signs I began to veer away from the ocean and instead to head inland into a labyrinth of confusing trails, footpaths, lanes and unmarked roads which crisscrossed the salt beds between Les Moutiers-en-Retz and Bouin. On a number of occasions I had to guess at which particular trail to take, it was pointless using the ocean as a guide as the trails aimed their directions to every point known on a compass. With more luck than judgement, I popped out of the salt laden maze at Port des Champs to once again cycle southwards with the ocean on my right-hand side.

However, my directional relief proved to be short lived and following a Vélocéan' sign I was again directed inland, this time on what was an especially narrow and roughly surfaced green-lane which crossed flat open farmland. The lane abruptly ended at an unsigned T junction giving me a choice of turning left or right; but which to take? I scrutinised my route mapping but its detail wasn't sufficient to be of any help, the junction wasn't shown. Looking eastwards I could just make out the sharp pointed spire of a church which I hoped could possibly be in the town of Beauvoir-sur-Mer. Lining Beauvoir-sur-Mer on my route map with the church spire indicated that I needed to turn left. Having no other reference I took the chance.

About 4km later my phone began trilling with a call from Fenella. She informed me that she'd tried to find me along the route, but hadn't been able to make out the exact direction of La Vélodyssée. She had however spotted a sign near a small white lighthouse at Port du Bec, where she'd stopped for coffee in a small café, before driving onwards to La Criox-Rouge, close to where the causeway to the Île de Noirmoutier began. As we talked another cyclist passed by, providing me with the hope that I'd taken the correct turn back at the unmarked junction.

By the time I'd finished speaking with Fenella, had a slurp from my Bidon, got myself sorted and back to cycling the other cyclist had pulled about 1.5km ahead of me. Yet, it appeared he and I were matching speeds, I wasn't gaining on him and he wasn't increasing the distance between us, and as we traversed the open lanes of the farmland his yellow cycling top was always easy for me to spot. I caught him as he halted at another junction. He appeared to be looking in confusion at the junction, the lane he'd just cycled and at what appeared to be a map in his handlebar bag. Pulling to a stop alongside I waved a cheery, 'Bonjour Monsieur', and that's how, for the third time, Hans and I met. I say third time because as we took note of each other, I immediately recognised him as being the solo cyclist I'd seen riding the Cube Touring bike way back in Brittany at Camping De Gouarec. Hans also recognised me as the chap he'd been frantically waving to from the top of the viaduct at La Villeneuve in an effort to indicate that the alternative route I should have been following that day was indeed on the viaduct! Talk about it being a small world!

I wrote in my blog later that day that Hans and I had met when we were both lost in space. Nothing to do with the crap film of the same name with some 'comedian' from Friends supposedly acting in it, and Hans being no relation to the other space-boy, Hans Solo. He was Hans Ghertt, a German cycle tourist, like me cycling La Vélodyssée, like me getting frustrated, like me lost in the space between the roads we were trying to negotiate and their pictorial depiction on our route maps.

The junction wasn't shown on either versions of our La Vélodyssée maps. Again it was a left or right choice. Looking carefully I noticed a small wooden arrow with the picture of a lighthouse pointing towards the right. Thinking about what Fenella had told me about spotting a route sign near a lighthouse at Port du Bec I suggested we take that road in the hope that the arrow was indicating the same lighthouse. With no other identifiable option Hans was up for giving it a try, and thankfully a few kilometres later we found ourselves at Port du Bec.

With that small success behind us, with an informal agreement based upon two similar aged blokes out on their bikes, both cycling at similar speeds, both riding Cube tourers and both without a firm commitment with regards to the days destination, we formed a two man team and for the first time on my journey I had myself a cycling buddy.

Following all those kilometres riding solo, oh what bliss it was to roll along the road having a natter, having a laugh and generally putting the world to rights with a fellow cyclist. On a 3 month expedition, traveling from Dusseldorf into Brittany by train, Hans was also cycling La Vélodyssée from Roscoff to Hendaye. He was also planning to cross over into Spain, but unlike me he wasn't planning to finish at San Sebastián, he was hoping to carry on to Lisbon in Portugal, a ride of about

1,800km, before catching the train back to Germany. A difficulty he had facing him, apart from actually cycling that distance was he didn't have any cycling maps covering Spain and Portugal, he hoped to purchase these in San Sebastián. If he was unable to do so he told me he'd turn tail and cycle eastwards through France, Switzerland and back into Germany, which would be still a hell of a ride. I began to feel somewhat ashamed at my lack of ambition and what I thought as my 'grandeé tour'.

Still, regardless of his intentions, knowing we would cycle the Île de Noirmoutier, Hans hadn't realised we had to cross a causeway, that at times, depending on the tide, could be underwater. Fenella and I had worked out that to safely cross the causeway in the afternoon I needed to be at La Criox-Rouge no later than 3pm. However with my very limited German, despite Hans' much better English, I couldn't get him to understand why we had to arrive at the causeway before a certain time. Also on reaching the D22, with our lost in space method of navigation, we'd ended up cycling in the wrong direction, and added to these problems the cloud had descended and it had begun to rain making visibility difficult. By the time we'd realised our mistake and turned around and met Fenella at La Criox-Rouge the digital display at the beginning of the causeway had begun to flash warnings in three languages, one being German, **'FLOOD ALERT- GEFAHR DER DROWNING',** 'oh my God', proclaimed Hans, 'now I understand what you were telling me'.

Following a quick confab about the safety of crossing, with both of us confirming we could swim, we decided to give it a go. Initially I led the way, perhaps because of the warning, I'd set off as if trying to make a breakaway from the peloton in Le Tour. The causeway surface is formed of cobbles, which as well as providing an agonisingly bumpy ride, with the recent rain had become extremely slippery, and with the pace I'd set we must have looked like a couple of madmen as we jolted and slid our way across. It was much worse for Hans, who unlike me, lightly loaded and carrying only a day's provisions, was riding with fully laden panniers, a large handlebar bag and a tent strapped to his rear rack. I needn't have acted so rashly. When I came to my senses and looked around, although hardly any traffic was on the causeway with us, at either side there were many folk gathering cockles and muscles in the shallow rock pools and a few were a good 100m distant burrowing for sand eels and other types of fresh bait. I reckoned even if the tide was swift as in many flat waterways, the locals would give us warning of when to make haste. We slowed our pace and began to enjoy the novel experience of cycling so far from land.

At 4.5km in length, Le Passage du Gois, to give the causeway its Sunday name, is actually a paved-over sandbank, and was the only link from the mainland to Île de Noirmoutier until 1971 when a bridge was constructed linking the south of the Île to Fromentine. Every year a foot race, the Foulées du Gois, is held across it, starting at the onset of the high tide. I'm unclear about what the winner of this race receives, but hopefully it includes a series of free psychological counselling sessions, as for the loser, it is to be hoped they are rescued before they swiftly bob away to experience the wild waters of the Bay of Biscay.

Reaching the Île our route took us along a series of unmarked lanes and greenways alongside the east coastline, before we merged with the D38 at Ponte de la Fosse and over the bridge and into Fromentine. Primarily a salt marsh with sand banks and oak forests, at 25km in length, because of its temperate climate which allows for the all year flowering of Acacia Dealbata (mimosa), a species of Acacia, native to south-eastern Australia, Noirmoutier is often referred to as the Island of Mimosas.

We remained on the D38 for the short run into the hamlet of La Corsive, where we entered the undulating Forêt des Pays de Monts. Rooted on a series of interlocking sand dunes, the recent rain had made the forêt going a tad gluey and with a combination of seemingly endless steep climbs and sharp descents the result was a tiring and trying ride.

Adjacent to the village of La Parée Chalon, stopping to gather our bearings at an information board, sensing we were both showing signs of energy loss, and realising I hadn't eaten since breakfast, I asked Hans how far he wanted to cycle before discontinuing for the day. He told me he didn't think he could cycle further than St-Jean-de-Monts, but if possible, he would like to ride until he caught up with another couple of German cyclists, whom he thought couldn't be too far ahead of us. Explaining my lack of nourishment, we had a brief rest while we shared my daily ration of fruit and nuts and an 'emergency' bidon of energy drink Hans pulled from his panniers.

Thankfully for Hans and for both of our wellbeing's, we caught his German cyclists in the forêt hamlet of La Vacherie. I could hardly believe it, the couple were none other than the elderly couple with their dog carrying all their gear in a trailer, who like Hans had also been tenting in Brittany at Camping De Gouarec. It was a day where my world continued to shrink.

Through a series of conversations in German, translated for me by Hans, I discovered that he, Walter, Mila and their dog August, had been crisscrossing each other along La Vélodyssée since leaving Roscoff. However, Walter and Mila weren't planning to cycle all the way down to Hendaye, on reaching Royan they planned to turn inland making for Bordeaux where they would catch the train back to Roscoff where they had left their car.

Upon meeting Walter and Mila I could see Hans was just about all-in. I had to remember that with all his gear his bike was much heavier than mine, but still, I wasn't too far off joining him in the fatigue stakes. Accordingly, at La Paré Jésus, spotting a campsite adjoining La Vélodyssée, along with Walter and Mila, Hans decided he'd had enough and would camp there for the night; he called it a day. I decided to cycle a little further into St-Jean-de-Monts where I would meet Fenella for coffee and a bite to eat. Hans and I didn't make a big deal about our farewells, we were both journeying the same route and with several hundred kilometres still ahead of us, despite scheduling differing rest days, we knew we'd meet up again. So with a firm handshake, a brief man-hug, and a quick 'Wir sehen uns später auf der Straße', Hans went off to make camp and I left to meet Fenella.

It had been several years since I'd last visited St-Jean-de-Monts and the place had certainly developed hugely since that time. The promenade had been completely restructured and extended with a large Ferris wheel holding centre stage. Fenella couldn't park her car anywhere near the beach front so we met behind the tourist office at the Chapelle des Goëlands where we could walk into the much quieter area of the Avenue des Demoiselles for late coffees and voileipäs.

Situated overlooking Lac du Jaunay, Le Pin Parasol, our campsite for the following two nights, was unlike any of the other sites we'd use during our trip. A large complex under the umbrella of the Yelloh! Village organisation it boasts many of the attractions that lure families from numerous European countries. But on the 12-13th of July it was still fairly quiet and peaceful, providing us with enough facilities to relax and unwind without proving to be too boisterous and bothersome. We made use of the bar TV, catching-up with world events and watching re-runs of the last few stages of Le Tour de France, cheering for Froome, once again wearing yellow, and to see Peter Sagan's astonishing assault on Mark Cavendish, causing him to have to abandon le tour through injury.

Lolling on the poolside loungers, sipping our beers and watching the sun dip behind the far shore of Lac du Jaunay, it was gratifying to reflect that the following day would be cycle free and even more satisfying to realise that somewhere along the ride that particular day I'd crossed my La Vélodyssée meridian. I was more than halfway along my planned journey. Clinking glasses with Fenella I voiced, 'more than half done, from here onwards it's gotta be all downhill, what do you reckon?' 'Yes dear', came her reasoned reply, 'all except for the Pyrenees'.

It must be comforting to be so wise.

With Hans at La Croix-Rouge beginning our
run along Le Passage du Gois to
Île de Noirmoutier

Following the previous day's squalls we once again awoke to clear skies and bright sunshine. But on that particular Thursday morning we didn't have to begin the day by preparing for our usual transient rush. A languid lay-in and a relaxed breakfast were the first orders of the day, followed by a meander to the pool area for a few lazy laps in the deserted complex.

I couldn't neglect my duties all morning, I had some serious engineering to complete on Pablo. Him being an equal member, I thought it only fair to treat him to a much needed spit and polish before I began the technical stuff. I realised that was perhaps the wrong sequence in which most mechanical investigations are undertaken, but I didn't want any unwanted debris contaminating my workspace. In other words I didn't want to end-up with acky mitts.

With all the accumulated muck removed from Pablo's wheels and frame, his handsome profile was transformed back to its stunning showroom fineness. 'Now for the 'specialised' manipulations', I mumbled under my breath so as not to upset him. Like all great artists at work I knew I had to progress his service by employing a logical process, so in the following order; I oiled his chain and gearing, checked his tyre pressures, patted his saddle and handlebars and confirmed him to be in perfect mechanical condition. Let me be honest, following the debacle with my tools on Pablo's pedals the last thing I wanted to do was over-engineer to the extent that more bits dropped off him. I worked to the old adage, 'if it ain't broke, don't fix it'.

Necessities completed we had the rest of the day to ourselves. We took a drive to nearby St-Gilles-Criox-de-Vie where I could have a splash in the waves while Fenella had a well-deserved lounge on the beach, reading, people-watching and letting the sun and ocean breezes ease her driving aches and pains.

Having cycled in the French heat so close to the ocean for many kilometres, on many occasions I'd been sorely tempted to pause my travels, run to the beach and plunge headlong into the salty coolness. I'd resisted. Still a vivid memory was when as a 12 year old I'd cycled with my best mate Paul to a park near Doncaster, which as well as having a large outdoor swimming pool also boasted to having a 'beach', which in reality was some leftover sand in a nearby disused quarry. I had a great time leaping from pool to quarry and back to pool. My last leap before cycling must have been into the quarry. By the time I'd arrived home the combination of wet sandy legs and undercarriage rubbing on a bike seat resulted in me having hardly any skin left on my backside and inner thighs. I didn't want to jeopardise my La Vélodyssée by skinning myself by jumping from sea to bike with sand still clinging to my tender most parts.

Meandering the town we called into a mobile phone shop on the off-chance that we could buy a charging lead for my GPS unit. We were astounded when showing the retail assistant my Garmin, in English he mumbled something like, 'ha ahh, an old GCX-HT-MLZ3, you don't see many of those nowadays, and now let me see'. He disappeared into a back storeroom where I could hear more mutterings and the shifting of boxes. He emerged several minutes later with a long charging lead, power unit and a French/UK mains adapter all connected to my Garmin. The whole lot only came to 10 Euros. Amazing!

The remainder of the day was spent shopping for essentials, relaxing back at Le Pin Parasol, eating and enjoying the odd glass or three of wine. All the while, as evening fell into night, we submitted our senses to our tiny 2 band radio and the ear-numbing discord fade of 21st century Euro trash. A perfect day off the bike, and instead, time spent together.

From St-Jean-de-Monts, along the coastline was a route I knew well, although I'd usually started inland from the calm of La Chappelle-Hermier. But from my starting point on that particular Friday I had to firstly negotiate my way along the harried ferment of the D123 to La Pège, before I could turn off-road and once more enjoy the serene shade of the southern section of the Forêt des Pays de Monts.

I knew I'd be riding this section of the forêt without my cycling buddy, riding Monday to Saturday and resting every Sunday, Hans would have cycled on my rest day and should be 60 to 70k ahead of me. Due to his organised schedule and my take-it-as-I-feel routine meant it was unlikely we would meet again until the following week.

Entering St-Gilles-Croix-de-Vie, along Avenue de ìlsle de Riez, opposite the railway station, the traffic had come to a standstill and a large crowd had gathered to listen to a military band, resplendent in historical uniforms. A number of the band members had gone a touch further and wore tattered liveries, some with fake bloodied bandages and a couple leaning on make-do crutches. Behind them, fluttering proudly against the cloudless cobalt sky was a large flag bearing the revolutionary corner stones of the French Republic; *libertè, égalité, fraternité.* Then it twigged as to why all the hustle-and-bustle, that Friday was the 228th anniversary of when Louis XVI asked a French duke if the storming of the Bastille was a revolt, to be shockingly answered, 'no, sire. It is a revolution'.   It was July 14th, La Féte Nationale.

Overlooking the steadily broiling sunbathers on the Grande Plage and a few optimistic surfers bobbing about on their boards in the calm shallows, braving the boisterous throng crowding Avenue Maurice Perray, I met Fenella for coffee, lemonade and a couple of welcome pains au chocolat.   We knew it would be difficult to meet-up again before Les Sables-d'Olonne, my route was largely off-road, whereas Fenella would be driving west of the L'Île-d'Olonne salt beds along the D38/D32.

Leaving St-Gilles via a stoned track closely following the River Le Jaunay until Le Pont-Jaunay, I then rode a series of unmarked lanes weaving the dunes of the Côte de Lumière (Coast of Light) and into the white bungalow metropolis of Brem-sur-Mer.

This area of the Vendée is aptly named, averaging 2,400 hours of sunshine each year, and regardless of wearing my darkest pair of sunglasses, as I made my way through the town the glare from the spiteful sun reflecting from the bleached bungalows had me almost cycling with eyes closed.

Despite the area's enchanting name it is a region that has been profuse in European history with regards to bloody battles. The term 'Vendée' has been used to describe the revolutionary encounters. The area also has a strong link with the history of Britain, being the birthplace of Eleanor of Aquitaine, who was married off to her third cousin King Henry II, and whose son was Richard I, the Lionheart, who took part in the Third Crusade and who features comprehensively in the Robin Hood legends.

Thankfully as I pedalled among the iridescent residences I wasn't witness to any bloody confrontations, although I did see two neighbours having a bit of a slanging match over what seemed to be an over-enthusiastic trimming of a dividing hedgerow. Hopefully this skirmish ended in peaceful accord without the need for one neighbour to make a crusade of hostility into his next door's driveway, or the marrying off of his daughter to ensure a lasting peace.

Tempers weren't the only thing getting heated, I was too. Since the cooling storm in Nantes and the squally showers when I'd been cycling with Hans, the temperature had slowly been increasing and was once again hitting the mid 30's. It came as a welcome relief to leave Brem-sur-Mer at Domaine des Granges Winery and enter the leafy coolness of the Forêt d'Olonne. However, one advantage the searing heat had produced was to bake the normally 'gluey' track surface into a consistency akin to hardened concrete, making the going much easier and quicker than my last cycle through the forêt, some two years previous.

Like in St-Gilles the Bastille Day holiday had brought the crowds out in force. Entering Les Sables-d'Olonne, to complete La Vélodyssée Section 6, there were so many folk promenading, and so many cars, enfolding irate drivers all searching for parking spaces I thought it would be impossible for Fenella to even drive into the city, let-alone be able to park her car and meet up with me.

Luckily, before our adventure we'd treated ourselves to a new Volvo, complete with an all-singing, all-dancing, voice operated media unit. Fenella was still grappling with the full complexities of this digitally displayed, Wi-fi-ed, Blue-toothed, female-voiced, computerised version of Orwell's Big Brother; a Swedish 'Little Sister'. But she had already figured-out how to instruct it (or her) to phone my mobile and her Scandinavian help-maid did so without any hesitations. It meant we could be in vocal contact safely and legally whilst she was driving, Fenella driving I mean, not Little Sister. As well as giving her up-to-date traffic information, including density of localised traffic, Little Sister could be programmed to pinpoint car parks within a given location. As usual, thinking logically ahead, Fenella had programmed her car to direct her to a small hidden away church car park and phoned me to inform me that she found a parking space. Discovering I was near the Tourist Information Office, on the Boulevard Franklin Roosevelt, via her car, she also directed me how to cycle there. Oh what a confidence building kick in the teeth; outsmarted by a bloody car dashboard.

Ready for refreshments we found a pavement table at a café adjacent to the Marina and while relaxing over strong coffees, we watched the world of Les Sables-d'Olonne pass by. Les Sables is often considered to be the 'nautical capital' of the Côte de Lumière as well as being the capital for tourism. The city has long been a magnet for tourists. The 19th century fashion for taking 'sea baths' became even more popular with the development of the French railway system and in 1866 the so called 'trains of pleasure' brought thousands of leisure seekers to stroll along the fast developing Embankment (seafront promenade). Goodness knows who the clientele would be if the French re-introduced the running of their trains of pleasure, although I'm pretty sure the rocking and rolling day trippers wouldn't want the climax of their excursion to be a walk up and down the seafront.

Les Sables-d'Olonne has distant roots pre-dating sun and sea bathers. Founded by Savey de Mauléon, Prince of Talmondias, the city had a commercial boom under the influence of Louis XI and his Councilor, Phillippe de Commines, who created the cities first port, trading in wine, salt and cereals. In the 17th century the port reached its peak as a hub for the cod trade, with more than 80 boats a year heading for the Newfoundland fishing grounds. This maritime tradition continues today and the 21st century finds Les Sables-d'Olonne to be a city boasting 3 ports; fishing, export and import and pleasure. It's a city seemingly in continual growth, a place expanding with repeated climaxes of embellishment.

Our campsite for the night, La Bolée d'Air, was a little further down the coast, at St Vincent-sur-Jard, hidden away along a quiet lane. But as we parked to book-in, in the distance towards the larger town of Longville-sur-Mer we could hear what seemed to be a funfair in full swing.

After pitching on the sandy ground, showered and changed, we found seats outside the bar and cooled ourselves down with a couple of Leffe beers. As we savoured our beers a rock band began to set up their equipment for that evenings gig. It was fun to watch, particularly since we'd often been co-opted into being roadies (elderly ones at that) when our son was a drummer in a local band. However, as we watched, commenting on this-and-that, it was obvious that, unlike the guitarists/singers in James' band, that group were organised down to a tee. No last minute panicked arguments about forgotten music stands, spare strings, guitar leads, and including on one infuriating occasion, the guitars themselves.

We dined on sausage, potatoes and French beans, washed down with a bottle of red and retired as the sun dipped behind the western horizon.

Then the ruckus started.

Firstly the band. They may have been organised, but compared to the band James drummed for, who in spite of their continual disorganisation, were a talented trio of musicians with an extremely respected reputation. But the campsite band were absolutely abysmal. I don't know if you've had the displeasure of hearing a French techno band murder British and American rock, but if you have then you'll know what I mean. Every version of every song came bristling through the night with a lead synth wailing away in strident discord to the other poorly played instruments and keening vocals. I say every version of every song because not content with murdering a good tune once, they played some songs a number of times at varying speeds and with differing interpretations. I thought it couldn't get worse, but around midnight they started 'playing' French pop music. It was like listening to a badly tuned radio at full volume. They quit their racket around 1am, only for the fireworks to start. They were then followed by a group of teenagers loudly shouting and bawling as they inexpertly played basketball in the nearby outside court. 'Bloody Bastille Day', I bawled at one point into the night, 'I wish I could get hold of a damn guillotine, there would be heads all over the bloody campsite come morning!' All in all a horribly disturbed night with us finally falling to sleep sometime around 4am.

On waking my first idea was to create as much clamour as I could produce. Make the bastards pay I thought, but I didn't have the energy, and when my head had cleared of drowsiness I reasoned, 'we are in France, the campers are all French, and it was their time of celebration, so I shouldn't really complain, well..... not too much anyway.'

Breakfasted-up and de-camped Fenella dropped me off at the fishery port in Les Sables-d'Olonne to begin La Vélodyssée Section 7 (126km) and what should be a two day ride to La Rochelle.

My ride out of Les Sables was, I believe, the most spectacular up to that point of my journey. A translucent cloudless sky appeared to drop to an ocean of royal blue. Triangular sails snapped in the breeze as masts bobbed the lazy swells. Swimmers and surfers shared a waterfront of silvery effervescence, while walkers and joggers of all speeds, shapes and sizes weaved along the Promenade Georges Clemenceau in their multi-coloured exercise outfits. The heady aroma of freshly ground beans wafting from the pavement coffee bars mixed with the salty freshness almost made me want to pull-over and join the café-goers for a second breakfast of rich-dark and buttered croissants. But I resisted. Instead as I crossed an arched wooden bridge spanning a fresh water run-off I stopped to take a photograph to remind me of such oceanic splendour. Framing Pablo in the foreground, and back-grounded by a chap who I thought was fishing for bait from the bridge, I snapped away. It wasn't until later in the day when showing Fenella my creative artistry and she enquired, 'why have you taken a photograph of a man peeing from a bridge? At the time I hadn't realised he was dangling more than his fishing rod through the railings, but I did realise that my digital art work would require either deleting, or if to be posted on my La Vélodyssée blog, some severe cropping'.

Once clear of the city the route became a tad undulating, providing me with some steep off-road climbs as I made my way through the villages of Le Village Du Bios de St-Jean and La Mine. On reaching the town of Bourgenay, La Vélodyssée splits which gave me a choice of two routes, one turning northward through the more residential areas of La Querry Pigeon and Les Brégeons, before looping southwards once more. Or the more southerly route I chose which wound its way through the maze-like oyster beds which pannier the Chenal du Payré à Talmont. The Payré is a small river that has its source about 20km from the coastline, but the sandy banks I was cycling wound their away across three small rivers that form the Payré estuary which shelters behind the huge dune of Veillon. The mixing of salt water from the ocean and the fresh waters of the rivers form a rich marine environment particularly conducive to the culture of oysters, and also making it a pearl of a cycling route.

I'd hoped to meet Fenella at the Port of La Guittière, the main port of Pays de la Loire for the trade of oysters, but the high temperatures and dusty trails had taken their toll on my energy levels and not realising my slow progress, thinking I'd already cycled through, after waiting for an hour or so, she'd driven ahead. I discovered later in the day her wait hadn't been totally in vain, she'd taken some very nice photographs of a man who was walking La Vélodyssée with a donkey. Which given how 'amazing' I believed my cycling of the route to be, rather put things in perspective, I began to feel a bit of an egotistical ass.

However, as the off-road segment of section 8 joined the D66f at La Fute-sur-Mer, crossing the river Le Lay, before I even knew about the walker, or could imagine how his ass ached, there were a few things I recognised for certain; all the previous build-up of kilometres of cycling, the days undulating terrain and the bumpy track, which had resulted in me bouncing on my saddle for a few hours had begun to make mine begin to throb. Also, despite downing as much water, fruit juice and energy drink as my bloated tummy could take the intensifying heat and lack of shade were causing me serious dehydration difficulties, I had begun to wobble rather than cycle my way along. With 80km completed I knew it was time to call it a day and I stopped to meet-up with Fenella in a large car park in a fly-ridden fish market, at L'Aiguillon-sur-Mer.

Under the vigilant scrutiny of an adjacent fellow camper, who critically commented to her husband about our every move, we set up camp in the town's municipal campsite, Camping Bay, and thirstily located ourselves in the bar. We'd timed things just right, happy hour. Although with Le Tour playing in the background and

Froome still in Yellow, on discovering we were British the barman/owner threatened, 'no happy hour for Brits, Froome no good!' Thankfully he was joking and we could sit drinking our Grimsberg beers watching our 'imported' Brit continue his dominance of what the French firmly, and often very vocally, believe is a race that should only be won by a French cyclist.

Not having had much chance to shop for provisions during the day, and the camp shop being on a municipal site not having a great deal of food items to choose from, we made do with a large tin of ravioli, a couple of baguettes and a bottle of undistinguished local red. Having mentioned the site being a municipal, it nevertheless still had an outdoor pool and a kid's play area, so it wasn't lacking in every respect. But a couple of items we'd both gladly have swapped the swimming pool for were toilet paper and loo seats. Bog roll wasn't too much of a problem, we had our own supply, but strangely when packing we'd forgotten to take a spare toilet seat. Without going into too much detail, when it's in the mid 30's outside, and you're a bit hot and sweaty, the last thing you need when going about your business is trying to balance on a slippery porcelain rim on a loo that's either too small or too large; to fall off, or fall in, that was the question.

Another aspect of the site being municipal was we were sharing a pitch with another unit, with the caravan and awning looking very much like a permanent fixture. While we were sat chatting and polishing off the wine, I noticed some kind of shadowy movement's within the caravan. In silhouette it looked like somebody waking-up, and despite the late hour, going through their morning stretch routines. Moving into the awning, the shadowy figure turned out to be a woman dressed in a sports leotard, and in clear sight her stretching routine became more and more vigorous and dance-like. She then ceased her movements and went back into the caravan, presumably to shower and change. While she was going about this two teenage lads arrived and set about getting a meal ready. Eventually, the woman, now dressed to the nines, and the lads, who I took to be her sons, all sat at a small table outside the awning to talk and share the meal. When I say share, what I mean is the lads each ate a good plateful of Spaghetti Bolognese, the woman, slurped a mug of coffee while sucking vigorously on a few hand-rolled cigarettes whilst moving her food around her plate without actually eating anything. Having finished playing with her meal, she gave both lads a peck on the cheek, jumped into a battered Honda Civic and drove off.

All the while Fenella and me sat rather quietly and without staring couldn't help but look towards the two lads. Catching one of the lad's eyes, someone had to break the ice, but not knowing what to say I tried an encouraging smile and a friendly nod. The lad smiled back, and obviously having noticed our car's British registration said in very good English, 'Mum has gone to work.'

Still not knowing quite what to say, I mumbled, 'ahh, yes I saw her doing her wake-up dancing, she looks to be

148

very fit'. Which thinking about it was not the brightest response about someone's mother, and perhaps I deserved the sharp kick on the leg from Fenella. But the lads either didn't get my vocal no-no, or chose to ignore it.

Wishing the lads 'au revoir', we called it a night and headed for the land of nod, both wondering about the woman's nightly occupation. Fenella thought maybe a bar person in a nightclub, or maybe like the character in the song by the Sheffield band, The Human League, 'a waitress in a cocktail bar.' I on the other hand had thoughts of her being an expensive escort to some visiting Mafia dons, or maybe a pole dancer in a seedy backstreet club, where the local big time money launderers meet up. Whatever the truth, about 3.30am the Honda returned and after a few au revoirs between the 'dancing queen' and her sons, the campsite returned to a municipal hush.

La Vélodyssée Section 7 route
map ready and waiting

Not a cloud in the sky as I leave Les Sables-
d'Olonne

All through my planning stage, if you could call it that, I'd imagined the weather in Brittany would be slightly warmer than at home, with it being extremely hot in the southern region of France and in Northern Spain. I had thought that I would be able to acclimatise during my ride. But it had been absolutely scorching as I rode my way through Brittany and along the Vendée coastline. However temperature-wise that Sunday morning in L'Aiguillon-sur-Mer took the biscuit. At 8am the car dashboard was showing 34°c and the car was parked in the shade under a large tree. I was in for the hottest day of my trip so far.

Back at the fish market, my finishing point the previous day, the bright sunshine, heat and the pungent whiff of fresh fish had the flies out in force. Annoyingly my bright cycling top acted like a visual magnet to the bloody things. Anyone watching me getting ready to cycle may have thought I'd recently received a short course of neighbourly pole-dancing lessons as I jumped and jigged around a La Vélodyssée sign post ineffectively trying to swat the aerial bombardment away. Although I felt certain that no one would try to slip a €50 note down the waistband of my shorts to enquire if I gave 'private demonstrations'.

My laughable pirouetting completed and a quick check that Pablo was all in working order, I left Fenella to seal herself in the security of her car away from the airborne wildlife, pointed Pablo along the Route de la Pointe and headed off.

Following the coastline through the villages of Les Glaireaux and Les Caves I turned inland through the unfortunately named La Dive, joined the D60 and cycled into the town of Michel-en-Herm. Turning right to leave the D60 I began to cycle through the heart of the marshland of Marais Poitevin, a great expanse of dry marshes towards the west and wet marshes towards the east, an expanse dotted with large commercial farms and smaller farmsteads. The area was declared a National Park in 1979, but lost that valuable protected status in 1997 due to the area's exhaustive agricultural development.

One of the choice crops of the region was sunflowers. Watching Le tour on TV I'd always thought what a spectacular sight it was when the peloton swished past those fields of gold. As I approached from a distance the acres of yellow certainly looked spectacular, but close up, and at times cycling through the sunflowers, provided me with a different perspective, they were literally buzzing with life. The kind of life that either wanted to bite, sting, or crawl their way into my ears, eyes or mouth. They were a crop best photographed from a distance rather than cycled in close proximity.

Approaching Marans, following the Canal maritime de Marans à la Mer, pushing my way into a strengthening head wind and with the heat gradually building, I began to experience more trouble with flies, but this time of a different variety and spelling. Because of the heat I was trying out a new pair of cycling shorts, mountain bike shorts that were much baggier and longer in the leg than my usual tight fitting lycra shorts. I thought they would be cooler and offer me more protection from the sun. When I'd first bought these from a well-known internet shopping site that shares the same name as a large South American river, they'd fitted me fine, but because of all my days of cycling, and although it's hard to believe from looking back at the photographs of my trip, I'd begun to lose weight and my waistline had begun to shrink. Annoyingly somewhere on the track adjacent to the canal my waistband button popped. Consequently, with the shorts being longer in the leg, and through the action of pedalling, my knees began to drag them down to such an extent the bottom of my flies were resting on Pablo's crossbar. To make matters worse, like most cyclists who use chamois cream, I don't wear underwear, I imagine I was anything other than a pretty sight. With no spare cycling clothing with me I had to continue to 'flie' onwards until I could meet up with Fenella at some point.

At Marans, passing the ancient watchtower on the estuary of the Niort Sèvre, which was once a lookout over the marshlands, I began to follow the towpath of the Canal de Marans à La Rochelle for a 25.5km run-in to the city. I was in a heat I'd never experienced before when cycling. To intensify my growing distress I hadn't managed to find any shops, bars or restaurants open along my route, Fenella's phone and mine were refusing to connect long enough for a conversation, and I was running out of drinkables. The juice I had left in my one remaining bidon was so warm it had begun to ferment into some foul tasting liquid that I'm sure could have acted as some form of potent weed killer or insect repellent. I was in serious danger of dehydration. I had no other option than to keep going, slow my pace down, chew on some of my energy jellies, take small regular sips of my newly fermented horticultural insecticide and hope I didn't fall into one of my 'collapsing episodes,' or I didn't poison myself.

Leaving the canal at Dompierre-sur-Mer, following a rough off-road track towards the city centre, I began to feel more positive that I was going to be ok. I'd managed to get in contact with Fenella, who'd informed me because of the heat she'd booked a hotel for the night, which she believed I would pass as I entered the city, and that she was waiting to meet me there. So, as I slowly dragged my weary body towards La Rochelle and out of the Pays de la Loire region and the end of La Vélodyssée Section 7, events appeared to be unfolding more positively. Little did I know what was to come next?

I entered the city along Rue de Perigny and on to Boulevard Joffre, where I hoped I could phone Fenella for directions to the hotel. But the area around the end of the boulevard was absolute manic. A large Ferris wheel had been erected and throngs of people were milling around, drinks in hand, and overlaying music was blaring out from a multitude of competing stages. It appeared the whole of the city's central district, ramparts and port areas had been transformed to celebrate Les Francofolies de La Rochelle, a festival of music featuring; soul, folk, hip-hop, electro, blues, rock, and all other styles in-between. As soon as I stopped cycling I was swallowed-up by a surging mass of overexcited and overstimulated humanity and swept along into the midst of their chaotic revelry. It was all I could do to cling tightly onto Pablo's handlebars and hope I didn't stumble to the floor to become a bearded dance mat, or end up being passed aloft, hand-over-hand in a heaving mosh-pit as an ageing mascot to the excesses of rock and roll, that was until I was abruptly disgorged a………..I had no idea?

After wandering around in aimless circles, overheated, dehydrated, dazed and confused from being pulled and pushed in every direction, I eventually discovered I was on the Quai Louis Durand. Phoning Fenella, who was still at the hotel and had no idea about the festival, I discovered I'd actually cycled past the damn place along Boulevard Joffre, but from my location on the Quai I had no idea how to get myself back there. We therefore agreed a good place to meet would be at the railway station as it would be well signed from all parts of the city, which it probably was, excepting I annoyingly discovered from Quai Louis Durand, the reason being presumably that not too many sailing craft travel by train.

Skirting the festival wasn't easy, it appeared to have its alcohol fuelled tendrils everywhere I tried to cycle, nor could I find a Le Gare sign for love-nor-money. I began to think that part of the festivities included covering every directional sign in the city. I even resorted to asking a couple of the music-revellers for directions, but either my French was so poor, or they were too pissed to understand me as they thought I was asking them for a dance. My temper began to be in synch with the heat of the day. The situation wasn't helped by the fact that when I at last found directions to La Gare and began cycling, I ended up on the city's dual carriageway ring-road and was given curt notice by the gestating occupants of a passing Gendarmerie patrol car to exit immediately, or discuss later at their convenience.

When I at last arrived at La Gare I couldn't find Fenella anywhere. On phoning her I discovered she was so worried about my dehydrated exhaustion she'd driven there so that I could load Pablo on the car and be chauffeured back to the hotel. But because the surrounding area was so busy she hadn't been able to find a parking space and was herself stuck in the one-way system of the ring road. She suggested I go to the hotel. The trouble was from my new position at Le Gare I had no idea where the hotel was.

The only visible structure we both could see was the Ferris wheel, so we agreed to try to meet there. Luckily Fenella was able to park nearby. But ashamedly by the time I arrived I'd gotten myself so bad-temperedly het-up I'd begun ranting and raving, even ready to blame Fenella for the troubles of my day. I was so hot and bothered that I rudely told her, 'sod this bloody place, I'm not bloody-well packing in for the day until I've found my La Velodyssee route out of this crazy fucking city.' Which in my irrationally bad temper I tried to do;

156

only to be sucked once more into the festival throng and spat out at the Quai de Durand. Which of course meant that the only way I knew how to get back to Fenella and the Ferris wheel was via Le Gare.....arrrh!

I arrived back to Fenella at about 6.45pm, but by that time my temper tantrums had ceased and I rather ashamedly slinked towards her like a misbehaving puppy with its tail between its legs.

On the way back to the hotel, once more past Le Gare, I noticed that the temperature, taken from a chemists display was an unbelievable 39^0C. Little wonder all the tanked-up festival goers were stumbling about like cross-strung marionettes at a Punch-and-Judy thrash. In their efforts to cool their thirsts with copious amounts of beer and other alcohol potions, they were actually rapidly dehydrating themselves, and the more they glugged the less alcohol their sweaty dehydrated bodies could absorb. I suspected many a lad-and-lass would have had a long, noisy, hot, vaguely remembered night, followed by an even longer, head-throbbing, murky morning.

In retrospect, I believe my own dehydrated state also played a part in my inability to figure out where I was in the city, how to find my way around, and how to find the hotel. I offer it as no excuse for my uncalled for behaviour towards Fenella, particularly when all her efforts were directed towards helping me. I will be forever ashamed. Sorry love.

Going on the recommendations given by the friendly hotel receptionist for a quiet place to eat that was beyond the city's musical ring of insanity, we dined outdoors at the La Marée Bistrot de la Mer, both enjoying the lip-smacking 25€ plat du jour of, Gratin de Fruits de Mer, Filet de Dorade Royal a la Plancha and Tarte Fine aux Pommes.

Given the almost suffocating heat of the day, after showering and a short kip, I'd lost so much bodily heat during my ride, despite it still being a warm late evening, for the first time since leaving home I'd felt the need to wear a long sleeved cotton shirt and a pair of jeans. While we were eating we noticed a chap at an adjacent table was also clad in denim, jacket and jeans. Fenella told me he was dressed in Valentino denim. That meant nothing to me, asking if it was good stuff, she informed me, 'yes, really good stuff, and really expensive. I'd say that his jacket and jeans would cost somewhere in the region of at least 1500€'
'Never,' I retorted, 'you can't pay that much for a pair of jeans and a jacket, no way!'
'It's true, that's how much they cost, I bet his jeans alone cost about 600€', Fenella insisted.
Good God', came my flabbergasted response, 'five hundred and odd quid, for a pair of jeans, and they don't look much better than mine at 15 quid from Matalan' (other clothing stores are available, but few have such a range of tack around the till areas).
'Well, I wouldn't go that far', muttered Fenella, eyeing me up and down a bit with a rather embarrassed look on

her face, 'especially when you don't button your flies properly'.

I'd known all along it was gonna be a day of troublesome flies, it had started in the fish market, continued with my cycling and ended in a fish restaurant. I reckoned events were telling me it was time to call it day and fly off back to the hotel for some much needed sleep. Hopefully sleep within solid walls rather than nylon, and without being kept awake by either synth-obsessed Bastille celebrating musicians, or probable pole dancers.

Part 4

Pedalling Poitou-Charentes – Boat On The River (Styx)

On awaking the following morning and venturing out into Les Rues in search of breakfast the streets had a much calmer air about them. Gone were the rowdy revellers and the city's night-time workforce had been out clearing the thousands of discarded plastic drinks glasses, much of the other accumulated rubbish such events produce, and we could hear the metallic clanging as the temporary stages were being dismantled. La Rochelle was being converted back into the city I had hoped I would find.

On that Monday morning, La Rochelle, La Ville Blanche, was glowing bright in the soft morning sunlight. The coastal gateway to Poitou-Charentes, first founded in the 10th century, the city was one of France's foremost seaports between the 14th and the 17th centuries. During the 14th century, and the Battle of La Rochelle, which pitted the French against the English, aided by the invaluable support of a Spanish naval force, the twin naval forces sailed out of the city's port and saw the repelling of the invading fleet.

In more recent history, during WW2, the city's port was used extensively by the occupying Germans, surprisingly the port, city and surrounding area suffered little damage by the invading allied forces and La Rochelle was the last city in France to be liberated from the clutch of the Nazis.

Today it is a haven of arched walkways, half-timbered houses, many protected from the harmful sprits of the sea by being adorned with gruesome gargoyles, and the whole is ringed by a wonderful array of lighthouses, elegant reminders of the city's seafaring heritage. It was a shame we didn't have time to see more, but La Vélodyssée Section 8 (145km) was calling me and I had to move on.

With the heat once again building I left La Rochelle via the Port des Minimes and followed the coastline until Pointe de Roux, before an off-road track led me through Aytré, along the stunning beachfronts of Angoulins and into the beautiful resort of Châtelaillon-Plage where I met Fenella.

As its name suggests Châtelaillon-Plage takes itself seriously when it comes to its beach, and why not. As Fenella and myself relaxed contentedly under the decked shaded canopies of café Le Grain de Sable we were both in agreement that as a seafront resort it hit all the buttons. Looking towards the ocean it was almost impossible not to be astounded by the beauty of the scene. The mesmerising blue of the water in perfect harmony with the cloud frilled sapphire skyline, both merging into the heat-hazed cerulean horizon. A backdrop guard of soldier-straight palm fringes created a cool avenue of green for the strolling players of this perfect seaside stage to glide through on their morning promenades. Not forgetting the beach, and what a beach lay stretched before us. Two and a half kilometers of deep, soft, light-golden grains, gently shelving to the calling water, protected in the north by the Île de Ré, and in the south by the Île d'Oléron; natural shoreline perfection.

Well, nearly.

The ocean and sky came as they were, but the rest was just about all man-made. Towards the close of the 20th century the town's frontage and beach were looking tired and dated. The promenade was spruced up, trees planted, walkways re-constructed, cafés refurbished and half-a-million cubic metres of fine sand was imported to repair the beach. It's still a nice place, the town is well worth a visit and it was a terrific location for us to converge, sip our coffees and make lose plans for the rest of our day.

Cycling along the Rue des Tamaris and then adjacent to the Avenue de la Falaise, overlooking the Baie d'Yves, closely following the line of the D137 towards the port of Rochefort, looking between the headland of the Pointe de la Fumée and the southern tip of the Île d'Aix, I could just spot the stumpy profile of Fort Boyard, that of the French TV programme of the same name, and forerunner of many similar TV challenge programmes e.g. The Crystal Maze.

Long before the French coastal waters were invaded by the English, in the irritating guises of Melinda

Messenger, Leslie Grantham and, if possible, the even more infuriating Geoffrey Bayldon, following the British Raid on Île d'Aix, after a number of failed construction attempts, under Napoleon Bonaparte's authority Fort Boyard was constructed to deter any further foreign coups along the coastline. That was until Channel 4 and Channel 5 made their financially inspired challenging moves.

Meanwhile, as I swung inland to follow the broad sweeping curves along the La Charente estuary and puffed my way in the direction of Rochefort, not to be confused with the place the cheese comes from, that has a 'q' in it, not a queue for the cheese, but a 'q' for the spelling, I was experiencing my own challenge. The physical challenge to keep pedalling. I didn't have any accurate knowledge of the temperature but the intense heat was acting like a physical presence, oppressively weighing me down with its energy-sapping heaviness.

For most of the day, knowing I'd be in for a warm 'un, I'd adopted Fenella's method of cycling; no rush, use an easy, even cadence and let the miles take care of themselves, rather than my usual rush and drop method of progress. But no matter, by about 2pm I was beginning to slack and I knew I was in dire need of re-fuelling, so leaving La Vélodyssée I took a detour through the centre of Rochefort. Passing a mini-market I bought a two litre bottle of chilled Iced Tea, two cans of undescribed cola and a couple of what looked like iced buns. Finding a tree shaded bench, in-between mouthfuls of sugary sweetness, I gulped one can of pop and a litre of Iced Tea straight down, before emptying my bidons of their warmed orangey solution and refilling them with a concoction of Ice tea and French cola. Not the best tasting cocktail I've ever sampled, but its E-number packed kick kept me going for a good few more kilometres.

Unfortunately, what it couldn't do was help me locate a way out of town that took me back on to La Velodyssee. Instead I ended up on the D733 and had to cycle the gigantic recently opened road bridge that crossed La Charente, only to discover the road then turned into a three-lane carriageway. Not the safest place on which to ride a bike. But no one tried to run me over, or even sounded their horns, maybe they just thought, 'oh, another Brit abroad, best left alone!' However, my inability to locate the route had a knock-on benefit as the D733 saved me about 15km of looping around to the west just to cycle the much smaller river crossing in the town of Cabariot. In its place I rode directly southwards into the town of Saint-Agnant, where I re-joined La Vélodyssée to follow the towpath of the Canal de Bridoire towards Marennes, our stop for the night.

Leaving the towpath at Bellevue I made my exit from the marshlands that I'd cycled for the past few days, saying my goodbyes to the rich birdlife that had helped keep me company on my passage through their homeland. It's estimated that the marshes are home to over 150 species of birds and offer a migratory transit site to many more winged visitors. Not being a dedicated 'twitcher' I'd been able to spot; herons (to me the greyhounds of the bird world), storks, geese, egrets, curlews, snipes, redshanks, lapwings and a huge variety of ducks including, eider, scoter, mallard, goldeneye (the James Bond of ducks) and the exotic mandarin. Strangely, I hadn't been able to spot any swans. Are you allowed to eat swan burgers in France? After all there's no Queenie to complain that the common folk of the land are snacking on her personal feathered fowls.

Having covered 80km I stopped cycling and met Fenella on the outskirts of Marennes in the picturesque village of Le Grand Breuil, where I could safely load Pablo for a short drive to our roadhouse for the night, an Ibis Styles hotel.

A fact that both Fenella and myself found interesting was the particular name of the hotel, not the Ibis bit, but the 'styles' part. Not that our room wasn't stylish, it was up to the job, not plush by any means, but pleasantly functional, having what would be expected in a hotel room; walls, floor, ceiling, window, bathroom, bed, although the cat curled asleep in the wardrobe came as a bit of a revelation, I guessed it must have been one of those little extra's that hotels like to provide when they go the extra mile.

After a touch of feline removal, and a welcome scrub-up, the evening meals we ordered from the à la-carte menu also had an unusual style about them, particularly for France; they were inedible. Although, maybe I'm being a touch over-critical, my starter of Bayonne ham salad was rather tasty, it's just a shame it wasn't brought to the table before my main meal instead of after dessert. Again looking on the positive side, our main courses of red-snapper had a distinctive air of, 'fishiness about them', and mine didn't move about my plate. However, poor Fenella's fish, being slightly singed on one side and a tad dusty on the other, gave her the impression that it may have leapt from the pan and onto the kitchen floor in an effort to make a getaway during the process of being slightly warmed. Unless of course it was trying to elude the cat. Our deserts were, we're not too sure really, as neither of us could quite face up to the two curdling crème brûlée plonked before us, particularly as neither of us had ordered them. Nonetheless, our beers went down fine.

Later in the evening, speaking to an English couple living in France permanently, we discovered they regularly used the Ibis restaurant, 'finding the food to be simply delicious'. Leaving me to think; where's a good swan burger when you need one?

We didn't have any further visits from the companionable cat and we retired in style to catch-up with world events by the stylish 'Americanised' TV presenters on the CBS world news programmes, and the less stylish French pundits of Le tour. Important to us was that both, using their differing styles of audience ensnarement, informed us that sometime during the following day the west coast of France should witness thundery showers, followed by a drop in temperature. Yippee!

The restaurant was less crowded than it had been during dinner the preceding evening, I hoped this was due to many of the guests not bothering to break their fast, rather than suffering cuisine induced eruptions of upset stomachs. Having eaten little we were both ready for food, thankfully few pre-cooked items were on display and almost all looked safe to eat. We avoided the scrambled eggs.

Back at Le Grand Breuil, unloading Pablo, temperature-wise little had changed, it was still sweltering and there was scant indication of any building clouds, let-alone the suggestion of the predicted storm gatherings. My first cycling task was to skirt around Marennes, cross La Seudre via the D728E, bypass the town of Tremblade and follow the coastline in an extended semi-circle through the Forêt de La Tremblade.

For a weekday morning the forét trails were being put to good use with joggers, walkers and cyclists out in force, many of whom I noticed were riding hired bikes with the logo, 'CYCLO TROTT' boldly displayed, all getting their daily dose of exercise. One old fella dressed in a long string vest, baggy shorts held-up by bright yellow braces and a pair of scuffed leather boots came trotting towards me looking absolutely exhausted. Yet he still had that determined look on his face that shouted to all who saw him, 'vous pensez peut-être que je suis démodé avec votre lycra brillant et vos entraîneurs de fantaisie, vous pourriez penser que je suis passé devant, mais je vais vous montrer ce qu'un vieux soldat peut faire!' Trailing behind him on a hired bike, dressed in bright Lycra and fancy trainers, was a middle-aged woman who could well have been his daughter, with a look on her face that said to all, 'Pourquoi diable suis-je ici en train de faire ça? Mon Dieu! Que se passe-t-il si le vieil imbécile le déchire ici? L'embarras de cela; Que vais-je dire à Ascelina et Madieu pendant le déjeuner?' I'm pretty sure that particular scenario wasn't meant to be played out by the 'cyclo trott' bike hire company.

I left the forêt at the town of La Palmyre with its impressive harbour and cycled along Boulevard de la Plage where I passed the frontage of Cyclo Trott Bike Hire, but I didn't spot any more old soldiers or their sullen shadowing offspring. Once through the town I re-joined the tree lined tracks of the forêt, exiting in the urban suburb of St-Palais-sur-Mer, on the outskirts of Royan.

Located in the peninsula of Arvert, on the right bank of the mouth of the largest estuary in Europe, La Gironde, Royan has a long established history as a holiday destination, largely thanks to its temperate micro-climate, said to be on par with the resorts along the Mediterranean coast. It boasts five beaches and a huge marina that can accommodate more than 1000 boats.

Originally of Celtic origin, with a peppered history of invasion by the Romans, Vikings and under British rule in the Hundred Years War, architecturally Royan, the martyred city, is relatively modern having been rebuilt following two raids in the early hours of January 5th 1945. When, at the request of Supreme Headquarters

Allied Expeditionary Force (SHAEF) commanded by Dwight D Eisenhower, 350 Allied bombers, with American B-17 Flying Fortresses and B-24 Liberators trialling extensive use of Napalm for the first time, is said to have, 'bombed Royan out of existence'. In total, 2,700 civilians were killed at the cost of only 23 Germans, an official report wrote that in all only 9 houses remained standing. It took most of the 1950's to reconstruct the city under an urbanisation programme and today Royan stands as a proud icon to 20th century modernist architecture.

Royan was the finishing point of La Vélodyssée Section 8, the last stop of my short pedal through Poitou-Charentes. Also, the point where many cycling tourists make the decision of either catching the ferry across La Gironde and into Aquitaine, my plan, or following the river down to Bordeaux.

Although we never met again, Royan was where the elderly couple, Walter and Mila, and not forgetting their dog August, would detour from La Vélodyssée, cycle to Bordeaux and catch a train back to Roscoff. It was also the place where I realised I'd never re-met Hans either. Which I thought strange as he planned to follow the exact same route as me, and despite our differing cycle and rest schedules we were both covering similar daily distances, passing through the same towns, passing the same cafés and the same campsites. Nonetheless, with a long way still left to cycle I still held hopes of meeting him again.

I met Fenella on the road to the ferry terminal, she'd managed to find a shady seat overlooking Plage de la Grande-Conche, an excellent place for me to safely load Pablo, have a catch-up of our mornings and just take in the view. It was a grand scene; the majestic Cordouan lighthouse, declared a national monument in 1862 giving it the same status as Notre Dame de Paris, standing stately and proud guarding the entrance to La Gironde. Ferries to and from Port Bloc crisscrossing the gleaming estuary, and the whole of Royan stretched out before us. I could have sat there gazing for the remainder of the afternoon, but as the saying goes, 'time and tide wait for no man', especially true for a plodder like me, and we had a ferry to catch.

Surprising myself by making it to Royan by early afternoon, and with a change to the earlier forecast, predicting storms for later that night, I wanted to make the most of the day, ferrying the estuary and getting a few kilometres under my belt before evening dawned.

At the ferry terminal, while Fenella dozed happily in the car with the air-con on full blast, I unloaded Pablo and meandered over to sit with the other cyclists waiting for the ferry. All looked to be tourers, but the disturbing aspect was at 62 and a half, I was by far the youngest cyclist sat there. For all the world it looked like we were extras in one of those annoying daytime, 'save the cost to your family and pay for your funeral now adverts'! As I looked over their various cycle's, and taking into account the number of prescribed drugs I carted around with me in case of a bodily break-down, I wondered just how much medication we carried around between us all. I suspected if we'd been searched as a group we could have been mistaken as being a multi-personnel mobile chemist; Boots on Tour. I'm sure I spotted a defibrillator poking out of the top flap of someone's rear pannier. I sincerely hoped they'd never need the use of it, or the need to employ it on any one of their travelling companions. Feeling dispirited at being at one in such company, I decided not to join them riding onto the ferry and re-loaded Pablo back on the car. Thankfully for Fenella, who's not at her best when using ferries, calm waters and a light breeze made for a pleasant 45minute crossing.

Port Bloc, at Le Verdon-sur-Mer, was the beginning of La Vélodyssée Section 9 (87km), and the start of my ride through Aquitaine, my last major region of France. After docking we didn't hang about as there was nothing of interest for us there, just a ferry booking office and a scruffy bar. My route took me off-road, past the Basilique de Notre-Dame-de-la-Fin-des-Terres, listed as a historic monument since 1891 and a World Heritage Site by UNESCO in 1998, and into the town of Soulac-sur-Mer, where I met Fenella.

Finding cover from the sun in a quiet bar with strong Wi-Fi we ordered soft fruit drinks, a large carafe of iced water and set about finding accommodation for the night. Our search was fruitless. No matter which hotel, B&B or campsite we contacted none could offer us a place for the night. We even asked the waiter in the bar if he could recommend anywhere. While he was pretending to think, a jaune femme presumably straight from the beach, dressed in a smart swimsuit came to ask for a table, to be curtly told by him that he wouldn't serve her until she was dressed appropriately, he suggested for his establishment she wear a dress. He was just as curt with us, informing he couldn't help, so we gave him up as a no-no. While we finished our drinks, having reluctantly decided our only option, unless we slept on the beach, was to return to Royan where there was more likely to be rooms in the city, the jaune femme came back. She must have been staying close by because she'd had time to change into a dress, cut high in some places, cut extremely low in others, with wide slits running down the sides from top to bottom it was a dress that revealed much more than her swimsuit. Without a word to the waiter she sat down, raised one finger, ordered wine and asked for the menu, the guy didn't know what to say, he just sulkily obeyed. I loved it. I hate restaurant staff who think they're God's gift to humankind. I remembered back to the 70's when Fenella and I were on holiday with Jay, our beautiful flat-coated retriever, a time when I had shoulder length hair, favoured cut-off Levi's and tie-dye granddad vests. Out walking we stopped at a restaurant for a bite to eat, having the dog with us Fenella went to ask if it was ok to bring him in while we ate, for the snooty waiter to look across to where I stood with Jay, turn to Fenella and say, 'you can bring your dog in, but not your boyfriend when he looks like that'. So for me the young lady did what I daren't do, she showed the stuck-up little jerk just who was boss. Good for her.

Her pluckiness didn't help us with finding a place to stay for the night and we had to turn tail, return to Port Bloc and ferry back to Royan, where we found a room in the Hôtel Arc en Ciel. Having booked the hotel whilst on the ferry back and having not seen the place in person, built above a series of pizza takeaways, burger bars and tacky touristy shops, we were a bit shocked at its appearance, but knowing beggars can't be choosers, we bit the bullet and walked through its doors. It was absolutely fine. Like the Ibis, not plush, but in no way pertaining to be 'stylish' either, then again it was respectfully serviceable and importantly, it came feline free.

We found a small restaurant away from the hustle-and-bustle of the seafront where we both polished off huge tuna salads, washed down with a Leffe beer followed by large desserts of fresh fruits and ice-cream. All the while being entertained by the second competent jaune femme of the day, this time gracefully practicing her acrobatics on a speeding longboard. It was like watching ballet on wheels.

Strolling to the shoreline, looking towards the ocean we could detect storm clouds rolling in, little by little the view darkened and an immense blast of cold air rushed inland. It took the seafront restaurants by surprise, awnings began to shake free of their supports, tables, chairs, menus, and even meals went flying in the windstorm. In the midst of all the chaos one chap still sat in his chair, with a huge grin across his face while his cutlery, pizza and table all took to the air. The reason for his happiness; from the cafés that the storm-front had hit first, where the diners had finished eating and had settled their bills leaving the money on the table ready to be collected, a number of notes had come sailing his way. A few had landed on his shirt front and stuck fast flattened tight by the wind. He was quid's in, or to be less Yorkshire, Euro's in.

We decided it wise to return to our hotel, sit on the balcony and watch the lightning spectacle out in the ocean until the storm finally entered La Gironde estuary and began to furiously pound Royan. It was a good enough hint to tell us it was time to bid the city goodnight and call it a day.

At Royan looking over La Gironde estuary
towards Aquitaine

Fenella enjoying the view at Plage
de la Grande-Conche, Royan

Part 5

Amid Aquitaine – The Sound of Silence (Simon and Garfunkel)

Third time lucky they say, we hoped so as we boarded the ferry for our third time. We knew it was lucky for the ferry company, they'd had over €100 out of us. There was little point in fretting about it, we had no other option but to make the crossing to Port Bloc once again, drive to Soulac-sur-Mer and re-start our journey. But one thing we had in our favour that time around was the weather. The storm had done its job and the overwhelming heat had been dispersed, replaced by sunny, but agreeable conditions, with the added advantage of a strong north to south breeze. It's hard to beat a back wind when on a bike.

Re-joining the off-road track I'd used to get to Soulac-sur-Mer, I made light work of reaching Pointe de la Négade and into the resort of Montalivit-les-Bains, where I met Fenella for late morning coffee and croissants.

From that point onwards, for the remainder of the day, it would have been hard to get lost, even for me, because my route was a single track concrete road through dense woodland.   Entering the Forêt de Vendays my road was so straight, apart from the 6 right angled corners I'd counted, it looked as if its constructors had simply drawn a north to south line through the forêt, felled the trees either side of the line and concreted down the middle. Which is more than likely what had happened.

Many parts of La Vélodyssée route utilises existing, unused roads, some of these are of German WW2 construction originally used for the transportation of troops and weaponry and particularly for the speedy passage of light vehicles e.g. armoured motorcycles and sidecars. With the western coast of Aquitaine having been within the German occupied zone, 1940 - 1945, I suspected the 21km route between Montalivet-les-Baines and Hourtin-Plage was one such section. It was refreshing to know that out of those dark days of occupation something that had been originally designed to cause social restriction had been renewed to give pleasure and freedom.

From Hourtin-Plage I entered the Réserve Naturelle Nationale des Dunes et des Marais d'Hourtin, which from 2009 was given nationally protected status by François Fillon, the then Prime Minister, due to the areas twin environments; the coastal dune system on the western fringes of the Landes plateau and the complex of wetlands on the coast. This montage of habitats make the réserve a rich region for the proliferation of a diverse range of flora, including protected species of hardwoods embracing the evergreen Holm Oak, sometimes referred to as 'holly oak', and Pedunculate Oak, a flowering European hardwood tree that can live up to 500 years.

The region is also noted for its richness of fauna. Reptiles, amphibians and mammals of the region include the European Pond Turtle, the Ocellated Lizard and European mink and otters. Due its geographical location, it is an extremely favorable site for the wintering of many migratory birds, such as Teal and Greylag Geese. I'd spotted none. In fact during my way along the whole length of the réserve, or the remaining woodlands, I didn't see any wildlife whatsoever. I heard plenty though, all of the same genera; cicadas. Being one of the world's loudest insects, with sounds recorded up to 120 decibels, I was cycling during the short period of weeks when the males spend time above ground contracting and relaxing membranes in their stomachs to 'sing' in the hope of attracting females. The forét's literally vibrated to the incessant racket of their singing.

Leaving the réserve and entering the Forêt de Carcans, yet both out of sight, I was cycling between two bodies of water. On my right, with a bass frequency much lower than the chirping Cicadas, was the booming waves of the Atlantic, a paradise for surfers waiting for 'the one', and to my left, at an elevation of 14m, was the largest freshwater lake in France, Lac d'Hourtin-Carcans, a haven for inland yachters, windsurfers and kite-surfers. Yet for all the possible activities either side of me, I'd hardly met anyone during the day, it felt as if I'd had that étape of La Vélodyssée all to myself, apart from the bloody cicadas that is.

With Fenella not being able to drive the forét's roads we'd agreed to meet up where my route crossed the D6 on the outskirts of Lacanau-Océan, the end of La Vélodyssée Section 9. As I made my exit from the forest, coming towards me I at last managed to spot a mammalian lifeform, a male English cycling one at that. I knew it was English from its attire; a multi-pocketed sleeveless cotton jacket, checked shirt, baggy shorts, long grey socks pulled up as far as they would go, feet in brown brogues, all topped off with a flat tweed cap, riding the classic British touring bike, a Dawes Galaxy and dangling from around his neck, the biggest pair of binoculars I'd ever seen. I had no hesitation with speaking English, offering him, 'a pleasant afternoon'. To which he repeated in kind. Once we'd passed I thought to myself, 'I don't care how powerful his spy glasses are, he won't get any close-ups of any wildlife in those woods, unless he's an avid cicada watcher'. But a hundred metres further along, as I ran along a tall barbed wire fence, I came to realise he could have been using his binoculars for some other reason. I was circling the perimeter of Camping Le Tedey, the largest nudist camping site on the French Atlantic coast.

Meeting Fenella at the junction at about 5.30pm, while I drank as much cool water as my stomach would allow, she told me that she'd booked us into a nearby Best Western golfing hotel for the night, as the only campsite with spaces was one called, Camping Le Tedey, which she didn't fancy. I never asked her why.

The hotel was hidden away in the woods, so still no escape from the noise of the cicadas, they became particularly rowdy as evening fell. Another aspect of the hotel that struck me as discomforting was the fact that it, and all it's associated out buildings were constructed from wood, no doubt fire resistant in some way. But I still couldn't help thinking, there we were at the close of an intense heat wave, in a large forêt, in which everything was tinder dry, in a wooden hotel, with only one access road leading in and out, which itself was closely bordered by woodlands. Which is why, as we sat on our balcony with a perfect view of a fire-watch tower a couple of kilometres away, we reported to the hotel manager the four youths who were in the process of lighting a fire on the border of the golf course and the tree-line. Who in turn swiftly alerted the Gendarmerie and Les Pompiers, and within ten minutes had the fire dowsed and the complaining youths led away, presumably to discuss the finer definitions of stupidity.

After Fenella had taken a dip in the pool, leaving me to sip beer and have a doze under the room's air-con, with no other towns or villages nearby we ate at the hotel on the outdoor balcony, having a very pleasant meal of pork steaks, creamed potatoes and green beans, accompanied by a tangy house white.

The whole complex, hotel, sports facility and golf course were almost deserted. Maybe all that dried wood had put folk off visiting. Only a few other diners were in the restaurant along with us; a dad with his young son, who looked as if they could've been on a dad's and lad's golfing break, and a young couple, who, from the way they stared deeply into each other's eyes, were enjoying a romantic escape, either that or they'd both forgotten to bring their specs down to dinner.

Returning to our balcony it all just about made for a relaxing tranquil evening, the distant boom of the surging ocean and the soft balmy breeze gently caressing the green foliage... accompanied by the bloody incessant, unremitting screech of cicadas!

As far as the eye can see, cutting a swathe through
the Forêt de Vendays, cycling one of the re-utilised
WW2 supply roads. Just me and the cicadas!

The dunes on the run-in to Lacanau-Océan,

Dinner in the hotel the previous night had been very enjoyable. The same couldn't be said for breakfast. A choice of tasteless cornflakes in one container or tasteless flakes of corn in another, we couldn't tell the difference, sliced bread that looked as if it had recently been used to wipe the tables and some strange looking and even weirder tasting cold sausages. After sampling a few items, we made do with luke-warm coffee and a few mini croissants.

Over breakfast Fenella put her navigator hat on and began to organise my remaining route cards. She soon realised I'd worked-out many of my last distances completely wrong. Some were under calculated, some over calculated. Not a bad average to my way of thinking. Fenella just sighed in exasperation and her look made me think I should go and find something I could manage doing without mishap. I gave the loo a try.

Choosing the disabled toilet I couldn't find the light cord anywhere, it must have taken me at least two minutes of agitated searching before I became sufficiently enlightened to go about my business. As I sat, fretting about my poor organisational skills, I was disturbed from my concentrations by a loud thumping on the loo door and frantic shouting in French. It seems I'd pulled the disabled assistance alarm several times in my attempts to turn the light on. I admit most times in life I do need assistance, but with that task I'd thought I'd been doing ok. To add injury to insult, in all the confusion I'd forgotten that I'd put my sunglasses in my hat, that was until I'd put my hat on my head to see them clatter boisterously around the rim before falling into the loo.

Once more in life, flushed with failure, I returned sheepishly to Fenella. While I'd been on my illuminating adventures she'd sorted my route cards and recalculated that I'd less than 340km to cycle to Hendaye and the finish of La Vélodyssée, a strange thought in itself after all the kilometres we'd already travelled. Following the idiotic start to my day I could do little except agree with Fenella that despite closing-in on the French/Spanish border I should take another rest day, allowing me to re-gather my energy levels before I began to cycle the foothills and higher climbs of the Pyrenees.

Back at the junction with the D6, the start of La Vélodyssée Section 10 (54.5km) I looked at where the track continued through Forêt de Lacanau towards Le-Porge-Océan and realised I wouldn't have to wait until the Pyrenees before my climbing abilities were put to the test. The route seemed to head towards the clouds.

Saying goodbye to Fenella, as I prepared myself, a young couple came cycling towards the bottom of the climb, the woman was riding a Dutch step-through with front and rear panniers, while the chap rode a French mountain bike, towing a trailer loaded with odds-and-sods of camping gear, two children and a small dog. The look on the poor chap's face when he saw the incline was worth a thousand words, all of them giving-out the same meaning; oh shit! He looked towards where I was getting ready and although it's probably wrong to even think it, I could swear he was silently imploring me, 'S'il vous plaît, pour l'amour de Dieu, emmenez un des enfants jusqu'à ce que nous arrivions au sommet, ou du moins, achetons le chien'! I could only give him a nod of understanding before I left and began my own assault on the hill.

After all those hundreds of kilometres on the flat, within no time every muscle in my body was in anguish, and to have both muscles in pain at the same time was absolute agony. But to my surprise, with the track becoming an undulating mixture of short steep climbs of about 14% and fast winding descents, I kept going and began to suspect I'd found my climbing legs.

I was still dissecting thick woodlands, I was still riding concrete roads I suspected dated back to WW2 and I still had the harsh din of Cicadas on either side of me, but I'd begun to encounter more and more cyclists and they all seemed to be Dutch. I'd figured this from the fact that as I'd skirted Le-Porge-Océan I'd cycled past huge campsites with a mixture of tents, caravans and motor-homes in which 9 out of ten vehicles bore a registration coming from the Netherlands. The route of La Vélodyssée between Le Lion and Le Grand-Crohot Océan, which encompasses Le-Porge-Océan, had been transformed from being French into being 'Little Holland'. Thousands of Dutch holidaymakers had descended along the 24km stretch of coastline to cycle, walk, swim and surf.

185

Two Kilometres after Grand-Crohot Océan, La Vélodyssée route splits into two, with one arm turning to run alongside the D3 and the N250, following the eastern shoreline of the Bassin d'Arcachon, through Arés, Audenge and into Arcachon. Or the off-road route I'd decided upon, following the Océan Atlantique coast to Cap Ferret where I'd planned to catch the ferry to Arcachon.

Almost immediately after the route split I lost the companionship of the other cyclists, it seemed the Dutch preferred to cycle the easterly route, leaving me to cycle the off-road route by myself. Once again it was just me, Pablo and the Cicadas. How could I forget the Cicadas? Since Soulac-sur-Mer, up to the outskirts of Cap Ferret, I'd been cycling Forêt tracks for the best part of 120km and during every kilometre of my ride I'd been deafeningly serenaded by bloody Cicadas, they'd just about driven me round the bend.

Therefore, as I rounded the last bend of the forêt track, leaving the trees behind to be replaced by the lapping ocean waters, the sound of silence that greeted me came as an acute shock to my system. So did the number of folk who seemed to have made Cap Ferret their destination for the evening, the place was teeming.

Another surprise was seeing a train running along the road. This was the Petit Train du Cap-Ferret trundling along its road embedded railway lines, connecting the beach at Plage de L'horizon to the Jetée de Béllisare, the jetty I needed for the Ferry across to Arcachon. As I approached the jetty, there were scores of people waiting for the train, more buying tickets for the ferry, others hiring bikes for the evening and the following day, still more jamming the roadside cafés and bars and what seemed like hundreds already queuing for the ferry. I thought I'd better not hang about looking around if I wanted to catch a ferry that evening.

Buying a ticket and joining the queue along the jetty I could see the Ferry as it docked. I was taken aback by its size, it was diddy. I knew it would be impossible for all the folk waiting to squeeze themselves on to that little vessel, I estimated it would take at least another three crossings before I would be able to board. What stunned me even more was the manner in which the bikes were being loaded on to the boat, they appeared to be being heaped together on top of each other in some kind of crude rack hanging over the stern. I looked around me at the people in the queue who had cycles, 90% of them had hire bikes and I reckoned they weren't bothered a smidgen about how they were going to be loaded. But I was bothered about my bike. I thought about how far we'd travelled together, how I'd looked after it, making sure it hadn't got damaged, hadn't fallen over or been scratched or scraped. Damn it! I thought of my bike as being more of a him than an it. There was absolutely no way I was going to let some rough handed deckhand chuck my traveling companion Pablo on to a rusting rack with a few dozen other bikes to be banged and bashed about. I turned and pushed my way through the queue and left the jetty.

Having cycled off-road all of that day, I was pretty knackered and I had no other option than to phone Fenella, who was driving the eastern perimeter of Bassin d'Arcachon at the time, to come and collect me. I imagine she wasn't too pleased at having to almost double back on herself, but if so, Fenella being Fenella, she never let on, she just kindly agreed.

Wanting to escape the crowds in Cap Ferret I cycled to the lighthouse at La Pointe at the very end of the peninsula to await my rescue. When Fenella found me I'd fallen fast asleep on a bench outside the lighthouse grounds. I wasn't in too good-a nick, but for the second consecutive day I'd cycled a complete section of La Vélodyssée, however it meant instead of arriving from Cap Ferret to Arcachon by boat, I'd have to arrive by car.

We camped for the night at Plage de la Hume, another municipal campsite. By the time we arrived all the local shops apart from a local boulangerie had closed for the night. We made do with a large tin of sausages from our reserve supply and a couple of baguettes with which we made hotdogs, some nectarines for dessert and a few cold beers. It was fine.

As I relaxed, lolling outside the tent watching the night roll in, sipping my Torq recovery drink, something I'd done steadfastly throughout my trip, I considered the fact that during the day I'd made a navigational error. Perhaps it would have been wise at the point where La Vélodyssée split outside Grand-Crohot Océan, if I'd taken the easterly route rather than have cycled down the peninsula to Cap Ferret. Common sense should have warned me that it was bound to end in failure when someone from Yorkshire, a cap and a ferret were all to be found in the same place at the same time.

But at least I'd completed my lonely sojourn through the earsplitting forêt's of Northern Aquitaine. I realised I'd still have to cycle more woodlands before the end of La Vélodyssée, but they wouldn't be the fruit-invested wooded tracts I'd just finished. As it was once noted by a renowned local of those parts, 'Les arbres ne sont pas connus par leurs feuilles, ni même par leurs fleurs, mais par leurs fruits', (Eleanor of Aquitaine), and the only fruits I'd known in those trees were the million upon millions of Cicadas.

It wasn't a bad campsite as municipal campsites go, but I didn't fancy using it as a base for a rest day. After a cold shower (not by choice, no hot water) and a spartan breakfast of nectarines and tea, we decamped and made our way to Jetée Thiers in Arcachon, where I should have ferried to the previous evening.

Beginning Vélodyssée Section 11 (202.5km), I left Arcachon following the off-road cycle path running parallel with the D218. This led me directly past La Grande Dune du Pilat. Due to its continual growth and movements, almost a living creature more than a large mound of sand, it is by far Europe's largest sand dune. Sometimes being referred to as, 'the menacing wall of sand', or even, 'the sand monster', the spectacular Dune du Pilat stretches along the Aquitaine coastline for more than 3km, with a width of 0.5km and reaching a height of 110 metres it is estimated to hold 60 million cubic metres of sand. Scientists believe the dune has existed for at least eight thousand years and with its side to side movements they measure that it is still growing at a rate of 5 metres per year, gradually displacing woodlands, roads and houses.

The dune has become a tourist destination in its own right. A staircase has been built to ease the climb to the top. Numerous souvenir shops, restaurants and hotels have opened nearby to cash-in on the dune's fame, although hopefully not too near, or one day they also may find themselves being swallowed by this swelling behemoth of sand.

Once clear of Dune du Pilat, my route crossed the D218 and closer to the Atlantique coastline. At La Salie Sud I was pleasantly surprised to find Fenella walking along the track. She had managed to find a lane running down to La Vélodyssée quite close to a secluded café, where we could sit and have a mid-morning coffee and a couple of delicious canelé each. It was then back on the bike to re-cross the D218 for my run-in to the busy resort of Biscarrosse-Plage.

La Vélodyssée almost led me to the beachfront, until I lost the route signs and had to make a number of frustrating excursions up and down side streets and residential dead-ends, before I spotted a local route running alongside the D146, which eventually joined up with La Vélodyssée. Having been annoyed at losing the route, my annoyance turned to despair when I saw my re-found terrain. Crossing a narrow northern section of Forêt de Biscarrosse, the incline was so extreme I wondered if I'd somehow bypassed a whole chunk of La Vélodyssée and had already hit the Pyrenees. Topping the tree-line, with some sections as steep as 18%, I was less worried about the possible din of Cicadas, I suspected they'd have had trouble breathing the rarified atmosphere, and was more concerned about getting my helmet damaged by aircraft coming in to land at the nearby Aérodrome de Biscarrosse-Parentis.

Thankfully it wasn't such a long climb and I was soon speeding downhill to skirt the southern shore of Lac de Cazaux Saguinet, the second largest freshwater lake in France. With a system of locks the lake is connected via le canal Transaquitain to another huge body of water, Lac Biscarrosse-Parentis, which when combined, the three together form the largest quantity of freshwater in France. I followed the towpath of le canal into the centre of Biscarrosse where I hoped to find a café or bar to have a small late lunch, but the streets were deserted and all the café's and bars I spotted were closed. It must have been siesta time. The only establishment that seemed to be open was the Art Deco film theatre, Cinéma Le Jean Renoir. Which to my mind should be dedicated to screening only Renoir films, such as 'Le Grande Illusion' (1937) or 'The Rules of the Game' (1939), which are considered by many film critics to be two of the finest films ever made. Instead it was showing, 'Spiderman–The Homecoming' and 'Captain Underpants'. I cycled on.

Joining the dedicated cycle track running alongside the D652 I had an easy going 16km ride through the hamlets of Capagut and Roupit and through the town of Parentis-en-Born to circle the southern shoreline of Lac Biscarrosse-Parentis. That particular étape was arguably the least scenic part of my whole journey, with just a busy road close to my right and scruffy fallow fields laying to my left. However, it was ideal for knocking off the kilometres and following my previous days of bumping along off-road tracks through dense woodlands it was agreeable to be once more out in the open.

In the town of Gastes I met with Fenella for late afternoon coffee and I wolfed-down a large packet of crisps and a ham sandwich, which was a break from my usual routine. I've discovered over the years I'm not a good eater when cycling, I find if I eat too much within a short period I begin to suffer painful stomach cramps. These are intensified if I were to have any energy gels or isotonic drinks. My routine is to have little snacks often and drink diluted orange juice loaded with extra sugar. Yet, the energy jellies Tony from the Cube store had advised I chew didn't adversely affect me in anyway whatsoever, and during my journey they became my go-to-snacks when I needed that extra kick of energy. My favorite food when cycling are richly buttered teacakes, particularly the currant variety from Rhodes my local bakery, which strangely I'd found difficult to purchase along La Vélodyssée. The longer I went without my teacakes the more I considered Rhodes' were missing out on an export opportunity. Nonetheless, my sandwich went down fine.

While I was eating Fenella searched the web for a hotel for the night. Realistically we only had the choice of a hotel back in Arcachon, or one further along the coast in Bayonne. As I had planned to cycle for only about another 15km and to have the following day as a rest day, with Arcachon being much closer, we plumbed for The Best Western Spa Plus hotel, located just outside the town centre.

From Gastes I had a short off-road section to the village of Sainte-Eulalie-en-Born where I again picked-up a roadside cycle way following the D87 to the town of Mimizan. I had hoped to cycle a little further to the coast, but fatigue overcame me and I suddenly had to call it a day. It would be nice to report that my decision to stop was based upon a rational self-evaluation of my condition, but I'd be lying, I'm not that sensible. Overtaking me in the car, and noticing how ineffectively I was cycling, Fenella stopped and told me I'd had enough, and being too knackered to argue with her, for another change to my routine, I did as I was told. Still, despite the lack of scenery I'd covered about 90km during the day and I believed I was making good progress towards the south of France.

From Mimizan it was almost a two hour drive to the hotel and well before arrival we were both in need of some good grub and a good rest. But as we pulled into the hotel's car park we wondered if we'd made a mistake. The place looked to be a huge rectangular concrete block, 10 stories high, located in a trading estate and next to a large hospital. 'Oh dear', I know we both thought, 'now what have we gone and done?' It was obviously going to be full of sleepless people, wandering the bleak bare corridors all night long worrying about their imminent operation in the adjacent building. Or the yowling relatives of Madam Toffléu on discovery of her ingrowing toenail.

Neither happened.

It was a wonderful hotel. We were in the purple section; I know that sounds weird, but each half of each floor was colour themed with colour corresponding décor and lighting. We had an attractive room complete with a small kitchenette, a larger than average hotel bathroom and a large balcony. After welcome showers we both enjoyed an exquisite evening meal of Paté de Campagné, with Fenella enjoying Beef Bourguignon, followed by Crepe Suzette, while I scoffed Fish Meuniére and Tarte Tartin, once again sharing the dining room with a couple who'd forgotten to take their specs along. All in all it made the perfect location for what would be my second day off the bike.

It felt wonderful waking up and knowing we had the day to ourselves. Having a small kitchenette in the room, we didn't bother with the hotel breakfast, instead we used-up the last of our supplies. With no time limits it was a morning meal that lasted up to elevenses, then it was time for a relaxed coffee and more snacks.

We spent the remainder of the morning having a wander around the hotel and a nose at the facilities. I didn't fancy the gym, I thought all that metal could be put to much better use than being hefted up and down. Given some re-smelting and a flair of craftsmanship there was probably 10 good bike frames in all that hardware. The strong smell of chlorinated water put us off having a dip in the pool. Although the coffee shop with its tasty looking selection of confectionery drew our interest enough to give it a try. It may be the case that I can't eat a lot when I'm cycling, but between one ride and another I can trough like a gud 'un.

Following a washing session of my cycling clothes, with the balcony providing a useful drying space, we then had a wander around the trading estate, calling at the gigantic E.Leclerc hypermarket where we purchased enough supplies to last us until the finish of our trip. Followed by a lazy afternoon watching Le Tour rider's battle out stage 19 on the daunting Pyrenean climbs of the Col d'Aspin, the mighty Col du Tourmalet and the final ascent of Col d'Aubisque, won by the Slovenian Primoz Roglic, with Wales's Team Sky rider Geraint Thomas (G.) finishing a magnificent second. I could only marvel at their cycling prowess and give thanks I didn't have to face anything like those climbs when I reached the Pyrenees.

Another superb meal in the hotel completed our languid day giving me the chance of having an early night and to mentally prepare for what hopefully would be the final knockings of my journey.

We breakfasted again using our own supplies before an early checkout and a drive back to Mimizan. Having treated Pablo to a clean and oiling on my first rest day I at least owed him a touch of maintenance following my second, so before commencing cycling I gave his chain and gear-train a thorough spray of cleaning and lubricating oil.

I was still following the D87 cycle way and I thought this would lead me directly through the town centre and onto Mimizan Plage, but it wasn't to be. To my frustration at the first roundabout, once more due to the lack of route signs, I found myself at a loss of which way to turn. Naturally I chose wrong. However, the players didn't complain too loudly as I crossed, double-crossed and re-crossed the 14th, 15th and 16th fairways of Golf de Mimizan before I popped out on a green-lane just before the bridge across The Courant de Mimizan and spotted Fenella's car parked outside Le Bar Thermal. She was enjoying a mid-morning coffee and employing the bar's free Wi-Fi to find a hotel for the night in Bayonne. I wasn't particularly ready to stop having so recently got myself back on track, but to turn my back on good coffee seemed too big a sin to commit, so not wanting to be dammed so early in the day I joined her and ordered coffee and sugared palmiers.

Leaving Fenella still searching hotels, having negotiated my way through a maze-like residential area I had an undulating 14km ride skirting the edge of Forêt de Mimizan and into the resort of Contis-Plage.

This was surf-bum corner. I don't mean that in a disrespectful way, what I mean is 90% of the folk wandering around near the beachfront looked as if they lived the biggest part of their lives either riding the waves, talking about riding the waves, or asleep dreaming about riding the waves. It was a life that in my late teenage years I desperately craved. But for a lad living in a small Yorkshire mining town 10 miles north of Doncaster it would have been no practical use for me wandering around town wearing faded Malibu's, a sun beached vest, flip-flops and carrying a smooth-waxed fishboard.

On that lunchtime as I cycled through I realised that the desire hadn't fully escaped me. Although nowadays if I tried to balance on a hurtling board I'd need an assistive hoist to help me clamber on top, waist high grab-rails to keep me up there, and padded water for when I inelegantly tumbled off. I thought I'd better carry on before the temptation got the better of me and I ended my journey there and then to live out the summer as, 'Hodaddy Poser', (the apt moniker a surf-name generator created for me).

Crossing the bubbling Courant de Contis I followed the line of the D403 to pass under the D85 where I found Fenella relaxing in her camping chair and reading under the shade of the tall pines. Both feeling the need for a walk, Fenella wanting to stretch her legs from driving and me to ease my saddle weary bum, I locked Pablo to the car's cycle rack and we had a slow stroll through the trees to Cap-de-L'Homy-Plage. Finding a corner table in the small bar/restaurant, for the second time over recent days succumbing to the enticing smell of food I broke my eating routine and went to town by ordering myself a Croque Madame with fries and onion rings, whilst Fenella ordered an unadorned Croque Monsieur.

As we were eating I noticed three well loaded dusty adapted road bikes propped together, whose riders were obviously cycling that section of La Vélodyssée. I didn't think any more about it until I heard a voice say, 'réveille Philippe, nous devons partir.'
For Philip to answer in sleepy English, 'no, leave me be, I need a bit longer yet, I'm still knackered out. You go, I'll catch up with you later'. Looking to where the speakers sat, it dawned on me. It was the three lads I'd seen just after I'd left the ferry way back at Roscoff.

The two French lads eventually managed to persuade the lethargic Philip into action and as they passed me all three gave me greeting waves. I wasn't sure they really recognised me, I think their greeting was more to do with acknowledging a fellow cyclist rather than a fellow Roscoff to Southern France Vélodyssée'er. Still it was comforting to discover they were still doing ok and despite Philip's afternoon drowsiness they were making just as good progress as me.

Finishing my unusually large meal, I wondered if I'd feel as lacklustre as Philip when I resumed cycling, or whether I'd pay the price of stomach cramps a few kilometres down the road. It was to be the latter. By the time I'd cycled between Cap-de-L'Homy-Plage and

Saint-Girons-Plage I knew my eyes had been bigger than my belly and that I should have resisted temptation; eaten less and drank more. It felt as if my front torso from chest to hips had been turned into an over-tightened drumhead. I felt nauseous, bloated and in need of a good winding.

Having experienced this before I knew the remedy.

Propping Pablo and finding a strong tree trunk I went through a routine of attempting to push the tree over with alternate stints of trying to touch my toes. Luckily, with the tree being far stronger than I and while I'm positive my legs have grown longer while my arms have shortened, meaning my fingers never quite made it all the way to my toes, my bizarre exercise programme eased my cramps and within twenty minutes I could ride again. I also resolved that while my cycling/eating regime may not suit everyone, even at that late stage of my journey, I'd not be seduced by the aroma of food and that I'd stick to eating my frugal rations when on the bike.

Once through Saint-Girons-Plage my route turned eastwards for 15km, circled the Étang de Léon and joined the cycle-way adjacent to the D652 providing me an easy 20km ride to Port Albert, located on the shoreline of the artificial lake at Vieux-Boucau-les-Bains, where I stopped for the day.

Fenella's earlier web-browsing had paid dividends and she'd found us a very pleasant, modern hotel near the river in Bayonne in which we planned to stay for two nights. It was an Okko hotel, being of French design with the intention of providing guests with high quality modern ambiances it was very different from any we'd previously experienced during our trip. Every aspect of the hotel was minimal, functional and worked perfectly. Including our room, which had a brilliantly designed pod bathroom constructed from wooden latticing and tinted glass. The ingenious twist being that from inside the bathroom it was possible to view the whole room, while from the room it was impossible to view inside the bathroom. It also had the strongest free Wifi signal I've found in a public space and I made full use of it downloading my blogs and tuning in to the BBC to catch up on events back in the UK. I was even more pleased to discover, as we used the lift, finding the Archers playing away for our entertainment. In the fresh evening air I was even more surprised to hear Eddie and Clarrie Grundy having a bit of a tiff on speakers outside the hotel. It wasn't until Fenella told me, 'it's not the hotel, it's you, you've still got Radio 4 playing on your phone in your pocket via the internet, duh'. Still, it was nice to catch up with the goings on in Ambridge for a while.

We ate in the hotel clubroom having a very enjoyable early supper comprising of French onion soup, hot and cold nibbles, salads, cheeses, meats and fresh fruits. All accompanied with complimentary beer and wine.

Sat in the hotel bar overlooking the River Adour I reflected that overall it had been a successful day. I'd covered 90km and set myself up nicely to cycle to Bayonne and possibly a little further along the way to Biarritz the following day. I'd re-met three cyclists who I'd first encountered in Northern Brittany. We had a great base for my final journeying through France and from the BBC I'd discovered that the weather should cool rapidly over the following days. It's just a shame to discover Eddie and Clarrie keep on arguing about the shortcomings of Eddie's dad, Joe, and that Eddie himself continually appears to have some daft scheme that Joe encourages him to pursue. I just worry that someday he'll get the crazy notion to try and 'find himself' by cycling through France and trying to cross the Pyrenees into Spain. Now that would be a daft!

Still on the right track

Coffee time at
Mimizan Plage

It was perceptibly cooler when we awoke. The seamless blue skies having been replaced with a shroud of scudding grey clouds, it looked like the BBC had got it right and rain was in the air. We had breakfast looking down onto the riverside where La Vélodyssée ran past our hotel and already in that early hour several tourists came pedalling by, one of them wearing a bright yellow top and for a minute I thought it was Hans, but as they neared I could clearly see they were much too young in the tooth. I realised that with less than 125km to cycle until I reached San Sebastián, at the most three days riding, if I was to meet-up with Hans again then time and distance weren't on my side.

We had a steady drive back to my previous day's finishing point at Vieux-Boucau-les-Bains, and for the first time since the day I'd cycled with Hans, along with my days provisions, I packed my rain jacket. If I timed things right I hoped I'd be back at our hotel sometime mid-afternoon where I could stop for the day and we could have an early beer.

Leaving Vieux-Boucau-les-Bains I followed a dedicated cycle lane running adjacent to the D79, which although it ran through the Forêt de Soustons the tree lines were a good half-kilometre away on either side. With the weather showing signs of change and the lowering rain clouds being driven by a strong northerly I was provided a hefty backwind tunneled by the bordering tree lines. It was like riding a power assisted bike, I fairly barreled along covering the 20km to Capbreton in just over an hour.

But much of my speedy travel time was lost while trying to negotiate my way through the town to rejoin La Vélodyssée in the district of Mengine. Where, to make matters more frustrating, instead of joining the off-road cycle way flanking the southerly route of the stream, Le Boudigau, I somehow missed the signs and ended up in Labenne, about 10km too far to the east. Not wanting to lose too much time doubling back hoping I could locate the signs, I cycled to the commuter district of Ondres and followed a local cycle-way to St-Robert, where I could rejoin La Vélodyssée.

The route ran through an industrial area close to the main railway line heading into Bayonne. I'd only been back on track for a kilometre when at a squeeze point a car and caravan unit being driven by someone who must have been deeply inspired by Dick Dastardly from Wacky Races fame, came hurtling along, his caravan bouncing violently from side-to side, and with only centimetres to spare nearly side-swiped me off planet earth. I'd have loved a stand-up argument with him, but before I could catch up, at a railway crossing Dickhead had sped off down a rutted track leading towards some scruffy industrial units. I got the feeling that if I'd followed him he'd have had some oversized mutant incarnation of Muttley trained and more than willing to tear me limb from limb. Not sure in which direction La Vélodyssée would take me into Bayonne City, but knowing the railway ran to the rear of our hotel, I followed it until I spotted the familiar silhouette of the hotel.

I expected Fenella would be there before me, hopefully having enjoyed a few coffees along with a relaxed read and a little people watching, but unknown to me, about the time I was arriving she was having a taffle with transport issues herself. The hotel had an underground car park, entered through steel shutters at the bottom of an extremely steep ramp. The shutters opened when a 5 digit personal code was entered via a digital unit located on the driver's side of the ramp. The trouble for Fenella was her car was right-hand drive, the digital unit was designed for left-hand drive cars. Therefore to open the shutters she had to get out of her car, try not to fall down the steep slope while walking around her car, enter her personal car park code and then walk back around her car to the driver's side. But every time she did this the shutters opened and then started to close before she could get back into her car. To make matters worse while I'd seen no rain while cycling, it had rained in Bayonne and the steep slope was wet and slippery, and although her handbrake held her wheels fast, inch by inch her car began to slide down the slope towards the shutters. Just at the point she imagined her new Volvo having its front end bashed-in, a French motorist pulled in behind her, entered his code allowing her to drive safely through. It was a morning where one French driver's arrival had nearly ruined our trip, while another's arrival had saved the day.

Following our dices with disaster we were both ready for a sit down and a dose of strong caffeine. I made mine part of a strangely unbalanced lunch of double espresso's, salted popcorn and mango yogurt.

Throughout the morning, thanks to the fortuitous back wind and decent track surfaces, I'd made good time and having a useful amount of the day left, whilst not quite basking in cycling prowess, I'd reached the part of my journey where I could confidently say from that point onwards I would be crossing into the threshold of the Basque regions of Southern France and Northern Spain.

Part 6

Progressing the Pyrenees – Fanfare for the Common Man (ELP)

Still in Aquitaine, it was only a short ride between Bayonne and Biarritz, but it was a huge distance travelled culturally. The small but perfectly formed cathedral city of Bayonne, the beginning of La Vélodyssée Section 12 (52km), sits contentedly at the confluence of two rivers, the Adour and Nive, as if to say to the world, 'hi, I'm Bayonne, I'm happy in my skin'. While the former whaling port of Biarritz and more recently considered, 'surf capital of Europe', seemed to shout out to the world, 'hey, look at me, I'm Biarritz, I've got the glamour and I've got the glitz'.

Bayonne's roots can be found stretching back to the 1st century when it was developed as a fortified enclosure by the ancient tribe of the Tarbelli who occupied the territory. Archaeological surveys have discovered signs of a Roman Castrum dating to the 4th century. Following troubled times through the Middle Ages the city became under English rule following the marriage of Eleanor of Aquitaine, to be returned to the French Crown after the Hundred Years War. The city witnessed a population explosion when large Jewish contingents fled to the city in their bids to escape the Spanish Inquisition (1478-1834), and brought with them a canny know-how of what can be concocted from the dried seeds of the cacao tree, they set about developing

Bayonne into the chocolate capital of France, a position it is still proud to hold.

Biarritz also has roots which can be found in medieval documents, including Baiona's Golden Book of 1186, being under the name of 'Bearids', and developed to be a fishing and whaling town until the 18th century. Its fame grew as a fashionable resort when in 1855 Napoleon III built his wife, Eugenie, a summer retreat on the seafront and the town became a favourite haunt for the aristocracy and their hangers-on as the place to parade their wealth. In more modern times, 1957, the American film director Peter Viertel was working in Biarritz with his wife Deborah Kerr on the film, 'The Sun Also Rises', when one of their friends from California visited the set and brought along his surfboard which he used off the town's beachfront finding it to be an excellent place to surf. This is widely documented to be the first surfing activity in European waters. During the European surfing boom of the 1970's Biarritz became the beach on which to be seen with a surfboard under your arm. It remains that way today. In contrast to Contis-Plage, less beach-bum and more beach-beautiful.

So a tale of two cities? Not in every respect. Both have rugby union teams that have dedicated followings and of more importance they are both immensely proud to be of Basque heritage and the two combined form the premier heart of the 'Pays basque français' (the Northern Basque région of France).

Edging the Bay of Biscay and flirting with the craggy foothills of the towering Pyrenees, once past Bayonne I knew I was cycling a different France to that I'd experienced to date. A country within a country. Populated by folk keeping Euskara, the Basque language, alive and well and being the kind of people who won't take any nonsense from anyone, regardless of rank or position. A bit like Yorkshire folk really. It seemed the further down the coast of France I cycled, spiritually, the closer I was getting to home.

I made it to La Grande Plage at 3pm, but on that day the ocean looked more slate grey than its usual deep blue. More Bridlington than Biarritz. Still, as I was sucked slowly along Quai de la Grande Plage with all the other crawling traffic, the surfers were out in force and as I looked towards the town my vista was of the three story Casino Barrier rather than the gaudy tackiness of Brid's JMS amusement arcade. The traffic flow was such that I had little chance to stop and stare, I was dragged along as if I was on an auto escalator, it was keep moving or be run over.

Climbing steeply out of Biarritz on the D911, the Avenue de Biarritz, I cycled a number of outlying villages including, Bidart, Uronea, Guéthary and Kokotia, all experiencing major construction works to the extent they were being ripped apart. I didn't spot any signs of a real community apart from a few old ladies standing in silent sentry outside their cottages, every single one of them dressed in black from head to toe. I got the impression they were in mourning for what, in all sense and purposes, appeared to be the destruction of the traditional in favour of the modernistic. I couldn't help but think that Biarritz was making more room for its growing glitz.

Detouring off the thundering D180 I found crossing the village of Erromardie to be particularly challenging. Dropping a couple of hundred feet to sea level, winding past a few cafes, only to climb back to my original height to re-join the D180, all within a distance of 1.5km, and halfway back up the rain entered the frame coming down in stair-rods. Dodging the early evening traffic I had to be extremely careful with my navigations because in a number of places the road merged with the E5, the area's major Autoroute into northern Spain.

Entering the outskirts of Saint-Jean-de-Luz at about 5.30pm, the telling combinations of the distance travelled, terrain and weather began to take its toll and I drew to a halt in the village of Haizé Errota, doubling back a couple of kilometres to the roadside Hotel Arena where it was more convenient for Fenella to find me. It wasn't a long drive back to Bayonne as we could use the major road systems, whereas on the bike I'd twisted and turned along the coastal lanes.

On arrival back I was in a confused mood knowing this would be the last of my journey's nights spent in France, as the following day I should make it to Hendaye, the official finishing location of La Vélodyssée. I didn't know whether to be happy or sad. Another issue niggling me was whereas I'd re-met a number of other Vélodyssée cyclists, I'd never re-met with Hans and I knew it was unlikely that it would happen during the 22km I had left to cycle to Hendaye. Like me he was planning to cycle to San Sebastián, but once over the border there were a number of alternative route options apart from the one I'd programmed into my Garmin. Still as the saying goes, 'the future is another country'. So, putting faith in the hope that Hans and I would meet up again, Fenella and myself had a relaxing evening and I mentally prepared for my last day and the added detail that most of it would be spent climbing from France into Spain. It looked very much like my future was indeed going to be another country; and a painful hilly one at that.

The weather was still on the pleasantly cool side when Fenella dropped me off back in Saint-Jean-de-Luz. I was anything but cool, I was totally untogether, probably more so than I'd been all trip. Part of me wanted to rush off and get it done and dusted, the other part wanted me to take it easy and enjoy what should be my last few kilometres. In retrospect I was trying to come to terms with a cycling undertaking that at many times had seemed to be unachievable, but now seemed to be achievable.

From a spectators perspective I imagine my disorientation must have been fun to watch. Unloading Pablo I popped him on his wheels, forgot to put out his stand and simply let go, I just managed to grab him before he crashed under a passing car. Three times I tried to attach my rear bag, three times it fell off. Although I did manage to attach my handlebar bag the first time of trying, but it was upside-down and my phone tumbled out, it wasn't damaged, but still, it wasn't the best start I'd had to a day.

Leaving Saint-Jean-de-Luz wasn't straightforward either, it took me several attempts to locate La Vélodyssée and when I did I wasn't wholly convinced I was on the main route and not some side spur leading to the town's indoor shopping centre. But then I noticed the direction the route was taking; up, up and further up, it was at that moment I knew I was on the correct route. I also knew I was about to meet my painfully hilly future.

Once across the bridge separating the port from La Nivelle river inlet there was only one road to follow, the D912 leading me along the beachfront, across the small stream of Ĺ'Untixin and onto the Route de la Corniche. Just as I approached the climb a team of five cyclists, heads down, arses in the air, eyes glued to their bike computers and all riding identical lightweight Binaca road bikes, came whooshing past me without so much as a glance. 'Show offs', I muttered to myself. But to give balance to the situation an old chap on a wobbly-wheeled mountain bike leaving a nearby supermarket gave me a huge thumbs up as if to say, 'Ne vous inquiétez pas pour ces twerps arrogants, allez-y moi vieux, vouns y arriverez', and so began the steepest and longest climb of my trip.

Without going into too much technical stuff about differing gearing ratios, I set-up Pablo in his smallest front chain ring, the third cog on his back sprocket and began to pedal. As I've mentioned earlier I'm not the best hill climber, but that particular set-up seemed to suit me fine and I found I was neither pushing with too much pressure on Pablo's pedals, nor spinning wildly without getting anywhere. I found I could breathe ok, my legs weren't giving me any particular pain and I wasn't desperately reaching for my bidon every 100m. In truth I absolutely surprised myself with my upwardly progress. For 20 minutes I maintained my steady headway. Even more astonishing, on the outskirts of Haizabia as the gradient hit 15%, I caught up and overtook three of the club cyclists who were showing obvious signs of distress. 25 minutes later I at last topped the climb in the village of Agerria and began a fantastically welcome descent into Hendaye and onto Boulevard de la Mer. Where to the surprise of many innocent bystanders I released all the tensions of my day, and probably of the previous 21 days, with a resounding yell of, 'yes, yes, yes, whoo-hoo! I've done it, I've just gone and bloody-well done it, I've cycled La Vélodyssée... YEA!'

I met Fenella at a small outdoor café on Boulevard de la Mer and we celebrated our success with double espressos and jam doughnuts. With sufficient caffeine in our blood streams we had a wander along the seafront looking to see if we could locate an official La Vélodyssée finish line or some other demarcation. But as in Roscoff there was nothing to indicate where La Vélodyssée began or ended, not even a rump-ripping old madam with a constipated poodle. Which in reflection is something of a shame, it would have been nice to have some dedicated symbol to be photographed against for posterity's sake, even without the pong or the poodle.

My day on the bike wasn't completed at that juncture though, I still had to get myself across the French/Spanish border and into San Sebastián. Having no Spanish cycle route maps, for the next part of my ride I had to rely on a route I'd pre-programmed into my Garmin at home using digital mapping. But in reality I had no idea if the route was possible to cycle or not, and with only one way to find out, I bid farewell, 'see you in Spain', to Fenella and set out to leave France.

As I cycled I discovered that Hendaye was turning out to be anything other than I'd expected it to be like. For some reason I'd assumed the place to be nothing more than an insignificant town, with the border being its most significant feature. I was rudely mistaken. Standing on the right bank of the river Bidassoa, which actually marks the Franco-Spanish border, Hendaye has three distinguishable sections; La ville, which includes the modern and striking Saint Vincent's Church and house, the last SNCF railway station in France and a large industrial zone. La Plage, which includes a large marina, the stunning Baie de Tixingudi and front de la riviére Bidassoa, and last but not least, Les Hauteus, a substantial and well to do residential quarter.

It took me a while to cycle Hendaye's long and winding seafront and it was difficult to determine where ocean became river. On the cycleway adjacent to Rue Richelieu I did however spot a view that was extremely familiar to me, the location where the photograph on the front cover of my La Vélodyssée Route Book had been taken. It seems the photographer hadn't travelled far to work. Interestingly although I'd looked at the book so many times and instantly recognised the scene I was cycling, it wasn't until months later when writing this book I realised I'd somehow fooled myself into believing the photograph was of a young mum and dad happily adventuring with their young daughter. All harmony and animated happiness. But when looking with a more critical eye I came to the impression the snap was actually of a much older couple with the woman seemingly berating the poor chap, who looked seawards with an expression that lamented, 'pour la femme pitoyée, fermez la bouche', while the young girl, granddaughter aged, looks heavenward in practiced despair. Thankfully, there were no signs of the mismatched trio as I followed in their tyre tracks and the only squawking was from the seagulls wheeling overhead.

Passing La Gare de Hendaye I came to the original Franco/Spanish border post which was firmly closed, shuttered and abandoned. I assumed in days gone by I would have had to join a queue of vehicles being thoroughly checked by a team of eagle-eyed guards overseen by gun-toting police. I merely rode up a short hill, past a bus station and a half-empty car-park and cycled the few remaining metres to the tatty border sign notifying me that I had made it to Spain.

Given all the kilometres I'd cycled in France, the low-key crossover into another country and the condition of the sign came as a bit of a disappointment. It would have been enjoyable to have had a little type of personal fanfare to announce my arrival. It was a shame my Garmin didn't recognise the borderline and play a short ditty of welcome, maybe a snippet of, 'Fanfare for the Common Man'. As for the Country sign I'm positive it would have looked more pleasing if not covered in graffiti and the demoralising communiqué, 'Cabrear e irse a casa'. So, a not so welcome to Spain.

Far more amicable were Milan and Tuur, two twenty-something year old Belgian backpackers who'd just completed a trip through central France. They were busy taking turns of photographing each other against the border sign and were happy when I offered to take a couple of snaps of them both together. They were also kind enough to save me the embarrassment of posing for a poorly framed selfie by taking my photograph.

While we were having a natter about our journeys another cyclist came speeding into the country. This was Tiago, who, while wildly gesticulating every direction found on a compass, vociferously informed us he was on his way home to Portugal cycling from Switzerland. Similar in age to Milan and Tuur his demure couldn't have been more contrasting. He was dressed in a filthy T-shirt and shorts, he looked as if he hadn't washed in weeks and every part of his bike and baggage was covered in a thick smearing of grime. He told us he'd cycled rough, eating in the cheapest places he could find, sleeping under hedgerows and slinking into campsites to use the toilet facilities. It was a crime for Milan's, Tuur's and my sense of smell he hadn't also slipped in a few showers while he was at it. He was so wild-eyed and so obviously spaced-out I'm not too sure he actually knew where he was, let alone what day it was. When Tuur asked where in Portugal he was headed, grabbing the poor chap in a smothering nose to nose embrace, in broken English he babbled, 'south, east, west, up, down. I go home, eat, sleep, jump on bike and go, maybe I go Greece, maybe I go Israel. Who knows, I am being free on bike'. Then releasing Tuur to suck in some much needed clean oxygen, he proffered us a cruddy wave and sped off on his dope fuelled travels.

When I believed Tiago had had enough time to get a good distance down the road and he wouldn't suddenly appear from a side road to tag along with me, I wished Milan and Tuur good travelling and began my run-in to San Sebastián.

On the outskirts of the commuter area of Mendelu I was surprised to find Fenella parked adjacent to the autopista, not what it sounds like, she wasn't desperate for the loo, it's just a great name for a highway. She was wondering if I was safe on the busy roads. I was, along the GI-636, among Spanish drivers, I'd found them all to be courteous and accommodating to my wobbly progress, but that close to the city with the traffic density increasing with every kilometre I cycled, we discussed the wisdom of me cycling any closer. I decided to give it a try, but 10km later the decision was taken out of my hands. In Pasai Antxo the already busy GI-636 merged with the GI-20 forming an expressway disappearing into an echoing tunnel beneath the river Urumea Itsasadarra. To my frustration cyclists were banned from using both the road and the tunnel.

To exit the roads I thought about climbing the embankment and scaling a wooden fence to a narrow lane running parallel with the road, but a huge dog was patrolling the other side of the fence, heckles raised and snarling in anger at my presence. It was large and annoyed enough to eat me for mains and Pablo for dessert. I was in a bit of a pickle. I couldn't go forward, I couldn't cycle back the way I'd come and seemingly I couldn't leave the road without becoming lunch for some breed of prowling Basque Beast.

Guess who came to my rescue once again? Needless to say. Fenella had spent a little longer having a read before following and finding me at the side of the road in my own confused state of autopisting. After loading Pablo on the car we entered the Polloe Tunelak Tunnel, drove under the river and popped out into San Sebastián.

We'd done it.

I hadn't managed to cycle into the heart of the city, but I'd achieved my goal of cycling in three countries and making it all the way to Spain on a bike and Fenella had driven, negotiated and navigated with absolute perfection all obstacles in her way, one of them of course being me.

We were booked into the Zenit Hotel in the city centre, which was fantastically appointed and had the added bonus of employing individuals with a range of learning difficulties in both supported and independent roles within all areas of the hotel. The Zenit organisation called their philosophy, 'Paving the Way', its aim being to help build a more caring society.

We'd just completed booking in when another trio of cyclists arrived, they were Elliot, Jim and Mason, hailing from North Carolina who'd flown to Europe to cycle in the Pyrenees, setting off from Montpellier to finish in San Sebastián. We had a gas about our adventures, me finding their journey along the mountain range an incredible feat of endurance, while they in turn appeared to be astounded that I'd ridden so many kilometres all by myself. But I couldn't think in those terms, Fenella and I had done it together, as a team. I may have done the pedalling bit, but without Fenella's organisational skills, her ability to see the wood from the trees, her kindness and her continued support I wouldn't have got much further than the outskirts of Roscoff, never mind into Northern Spain. No, even when I'd been by myself, I'd never been alone.

During the evening we didn't venture much further than the Zenit, spending our time sipping cold Spanish beer, dining in the hotel restaurant and catching up with friends and family via social media and I took the opportunity of uploading a few outstanding blogs to my La Vélodyssée site.

In many respects although I felt slightly smug at having completed the whole distance in 21 cycling days, I also remember feeling somewhat ill at ease that my adventure had ended. Having spent so much brain power thinking about having a crack at La Velodyssee, followed by all the energy I'd invested when on the bike, ticking the kilometres off one-by-one with the hope of eventual completion, and then having achieved it, as I relaxed in the bar that evening I remember thinking.....now what?

We also had a lengthier natter with Elliot, Jim and Mason, discovering they'd used the credit card method of cycle touring. Carrying nothing but the bare essentials they'd bought everything they needed as they travelled, paying hotels to clean their cycling clothes, using bike shops for cycle maintenance and relying on mobile phone mapping apps for plotting and navigating routes. Unlike me they'd set fixed daily distance goals and taken their journey to be a challenge against the clock rather than a trip to be savoured for itself. I was in no position to criticise, in the past I'd been there, I'd done that and I'd paid the price of absolute exhaustion and looked the way they began to look as the evening unfolded. They had to leave San Sebastián the following day, relying on the post office in Montpellier to post their cycle boxes on to the Zenit Hotel so they could dismantle their bikes in preparation for their flights back to the States later that evening. For Fenella and me we had plans to spend a day or two exploring what the city had to offer to two weary, but somewhat proud long distance travellers.

I never did re-meet Hans.

Feeling a little smug with myself on the completion of La Vélodyssée at the beachfront in Hendaye with Spain in the background

Reflections

You Can't Always Get What You Want (The Rolling Stones)

We spent the following morning having a wander around the city before returning to the hotel for lunch. We discovered Elliot and Mason in the throes of dismantling their cycles and packing them securely in specially made cycle boxes. Asking if Jim had already finished, giving a grimace of concern Mason pointed to a battered shoe box resting against a litter bin and confided, 'unfortunately not. The post office in Montpellier, instead of posting him his bike box posted him that damn thing next to the bin. To make matters worse inside it he found a postcard pinned to the top of a pink hand-knitted dolls jumper with the inscription, 'J'espère que c'est la bonne taille pour vous'. Jims' livid. He's ended up with a dolls jumper in a tatty shoe box, while somebody somewhere has his bike box. The post office swear it wasn't their doing, what can you say?'
'Where is he, what's he going to do?' asked Fenella.
'He's out on his bike trying to find a bike shop that can sell him a box', answered Elliot. 'But even if he finds one, he's gonna be pushed to dismantle his bike in time to catch the train to the airport for the flight'.
'Oh no', was all I could think of to say, then added, 'if there's anything we can do to help please let us know, we have a car if that's of any use'. We'll just be inside having a bite to eat, come and find us'.

Thanking us, we left Mason and Elliot to their tasks in the hope that the third member of their team could sort things out in time. They didn't come to find us over lunch and when we left the hotel in mid-afternoon neither Mason, Elliot nor Jim could be found. We could only hope that Jim had got himself sorted and had managed to make his travel connections.

We enjoyed the rest of the afternoon on the beach dozing in the Spanish warmth interspersed with refreshing dips in the cooling ocean. If you're ever in the San Sebastián area I highly recommend spending a little time on one of the three golden beaches that grace the city's shorefront, in many reviews they are constantly considered to be in the top ten beaches worldwide.

Arriving back at the hotel we found Jim at the reception desk booking himself another room for the night. It had appeared events hadn't worked out for him. He'd managed to buy himself a bike box and with the help of Mason and Elliot he'd got his bike dismantled and packed in time to catch the train to the airport, only to discover his box was considered too large to be loaded onto the aeroplane. He'd had to return to the Zenit and arrange for the FedEx postal service to transport his bike back to the States. Sadly he told us, the cost of the return fare for his bike, plus the price of the bike box and his rearranged flight came to far more than his bike was actually worth, but after all his troubles there was no way he was leaving his bike behind. Poor Jim.

That bit of drama didn't prove to be the last of our trip. We spent the following day enjoying more of San Sebastián before beginning a leisurely drive back through France via the Dordogne, to spend five days camping in the Loire Valley. But when staying in a hotel in Bergerac, one morning before we awoke, some Swedish twit ran into the back of Fenella's car. Luckily for her, the cycle rack took all the damage, and luckily for me, Pablo was unloaded at the time. Despite broken light lenses and bent metalwork the electrics on the rack worked ok, but I still had to spend a good part of that morning with rolls of insulating tape and bits of wood performing a bodge job to be able to safely load my bike. The guy left his email details at the hotel reception and pledged to pay for the damages, but on returning home and making contact with him he never made true his promises. After all the cofufle with bike racks on our day of departure, and the purchase of that particular model, it was ironic to journey back to the UK with such a dilapidated bit of metal and plastic hanging on the back of Fenella's car.

So, after all the event-free cycling and driving through France the last days of our trip proved to be a catalogue of unfortunate postage errors, mis-understood sizing that finally ended with a bit of auto bish-bash. Not exactly what we wanted, but as the Stones remind us, 'You can't always get what you want', and who's going to argue with them.

Back in the UK, with a bit of time having passed since our La Vélodyssée I had a chance to reflect on our trip and ask myself a few questions:

Was it all worth it?
Was it enjoyable?
Would I do it again?
What next?

Yes, I think it was worth it. I had always wanted to complete a long cycle ride on the continent and France was always to be my choice of destination. On top of that I'd long wanted to cycle the Devon Coast to Coast cycle route, so to complete both in one trip made my venture worth it. Of course that's a purely selfish answer without taking Fenella's considerations into account, although she has told me she too found the trip a worthwhile experience. As well as the cycling we had the opportunity of spending a month together, visiting new destinations and being somewhat removed from the everyday concerns that often seem so vastly important, that is until you leave them behind to concentrate with discovering new horizons. I'd also discovered and embraced for what is to me a new and 'scientific' approach to energy sustainment and recovery by taking Tony's (Cube Store, Scunthorpe) advice when cycling, by chewing regularly on isotonic jellies, and at the close of each day drinking his highly recommended Torq recovery supplement. Which are dietary methods that I'll continue to use during any further cycling adventures. Not forgetting of course that one of my main aims of the trip was to raise money for the

Yorkshire Cancer Research, and I'm pleased to say that by the time I'd reached Spain my target had been met and almost doubled. Many thanks to all who donated and for those who still wish to donate to this fantastic charity please visit: www.justgiving.com/account/your-pages/Mike-Banks4

Most of it was enjoyable. I particularly loved cycling in France where cyclists are respected and given due consideration as valued road users. Fenella also enjoys driving and loved driving on the much quieter roadways of France. However, with the biggest percent of my cycling completed off-road on forest tracks, by the time I'd made Spain I was bruised from my upper thighs to the small of my back and I must admit that wasn't a particularly enjoyable experience. But on the other hand it was enjoyable to have completed the whole journey without injury or illness. It was particularly enjoyable not to have experienced any of my collapses and know, unlike on my LEJOG ride, that I seemed to be ok with cycling such distances once again.

No, I wouldn't cycle La Vélodyssée again. In conjunction with the philosophy of, 'once done, best left done', I was disappointed with much of the La Vélodyssée route. When forming the idea to cycle down the west coast of France I'd always imagined cycling for kilometre after kilometre against the blue backdrop of a surging ocean. It didn't work out that way. I relished cycling against the ocean shoreline in the Northern Vendee and from Bayonne to Hendaye, but I spent so many kilometres cycling through woodlands with the harsh racket of cicadas ringing in my ears by the time I'd left the large forests of Southern Aquitaine I was sick to my back teeth of seeing bloody trees. Also, there's so many more places in both the UK and worldwide to discover, so why do the same thing over again?

But what next is a tricky one. I would love to cycle different regions of France and to cycle in a number of other countries. Yet, there is still a great deal more for me to discover by cycling in the UK. Nonetheless, I have the germ of an idea ticking away in the back of my mind. When I'd set out to cycle and write about my adventures my dream was always to create a trilogy of books. My first book, 'More Than The Bike' is already out there and details my Land's End to John o'Groats cycle trip on my bike, Rocky, and as this book is about myself and my bike Pablo, for my third book, despite Rocky being a tad on the small side, I can imagine planning a trip that would involve using both bikes. Not at the same time, but completing one half of the trip on one bike and the other half on the other. But who knows? As I've mentioned before because the future is another country, at the moment I can only look at my bikes and ask myself.....so then Michael, is it going to be Rocky, is it going to be Pablo, or is it going to be both of them, and when you've made your mind up about that quandary; which country is going to be your future?

I'll let you know.

Appendix I

La Vélodyssée Blogs

27 December 2016

So as 2017 approaches I can begin planning my next solo cycling trip, (solo in the sense that I do the pedalling, while Fenella does the driving, accurate planning and no-nonsense reasoning) which if all goes to plan should see me cycle firstly in the south west of England, then along the west coast of France to finish with a little climbing to initially tip my front wheel into Spain. Which to my reckoning should take me around 1000 miles.

As often is the case I believed I could manage to navigate my way along the route with little difficulties, I do have these misleading thoughts from time to time, but Fenella, blessed with a thinking unit that runs on rather smoother roads than mine had other ideas. Therefore, to keep me generally on the right track she has invested in some Christmas present insurance, namely in the form of an up-to-date French road map, a detailed stage-by stage route guide and a cycle Garmin GPS sat nav unit with European mapping.

Bring on being lost abroad, (which is a country I can't find in my atlas...is in under 'A' in the index?).

2 March 2017

What is it with the Belgians?

What makes them so outwardly awkward? Awkward in a 'standoffish', scared, don't-look-at-me-mate sort of way. Just what is it that wobbles their mantel? Is it the making of eye contact, is it that in Belgium to smile is to make a rude gesture, or is it they have an in-built inherent mistrust of strangers? Could it be that in the past these advocates of modern Europe have been so let down by 'dangerous foreigners' that when they meet a duo of folk who hail from across their borders, even though these folk are man and wife, in their 60's, on bikes and are obviously knackered and hopelessly lost, the lone Belgian whom has been asked for directions, can't help but grimace, turn their head and following a second or two's indecision, scuttle hurriedly away with the fearful thought of, 'oh no, not another bloody invasion'!

I think I'd better explain why I ask.

It all began with an ending, as most beginnings I know tend to do. As a few of you may already know, a couple of years ago in my book, More Than the Bike, I told of what I called my 'Summer of Madness', which began with me completing my first triathlon, a Lands End to John O'Groats cycle ride and ended, following my entry into the Great North Run and a late autumn cycle ride, with me in a hospital bed in that great Yorkshire city of Kingston Upon Hull.

This was followed by a couple of years of medical tests, and enforced rests from further dabbles into the world of sports. However, as I slowly recovered my equilibrium and my self-confinement away from the bike, I began to start having thoughts of another long distance cycle adventure, this time a jaunt somewhere in Europe rather than within the confines of the UK. I started to form the idea of cycling through France and then hopping across the border into Northern Spain. But, even a fool like me realised, after being 'ill' on and off for nearly two years, I just couldn't jump back on my bike, wave 'cheerio' to family and friends, and merrily tootle off down the road towards the south coast ferry ports. No, I knew I needed to train my way back towards a semblance of fitness, slowly, sensibly (difficult for me I know) and over a reasonably long period of time. I also reckoned it may be advantageous to my training to include a cycle trip at least somewhere in Europe. I recognised before I headed for France and Spain I had to get my legs used to cycling again, and I also knew these pair of muscle-free body-hindrances would need a lot of coaxing, and to be honest a fair amount of deception, before they began to remotely resemble limbs strong enough to cycle around a thousand miles or so.

Therefore, if fooling them into believing I was going to take them on holiday to Belgium and Holland would help me with this task, so be it, I just didn't mention to them it was to be a cycling holiday.

And so our meetings with Belgians began.

14 April 2017

Ahh Belgium.

A fantastic place to cycle, fantastic cities and towns to visit, fantastic countryside, and fantastic traffic-free interlacing cycle-ways, all populated with…..Belgians.

Maybe they're great folk, maybe they're friendly, warm, fantastically hospitable people. It could be I'm being a bit too down on them. I guess it could be I've got them totally wrong. But if so, all those welcoming, responsive, cordial individuals must have been hiding indoors, curtains and shutters firmly barred and TV blaring loudly to minimise the chances of being disturbed by a couple of transient elderly English cyclists passing through their neighbourhood, or God forbid they may have had to acknowledge them. Not that we intended to knock on any doors seeking any kind of communication. No, all we attempted to do was greet our fellow cyclists and passers-by's with a cheery 'geode morgen, goedenmiddag', or even a quiet 'hallo'; but all we got in return, at least 90% of the time, was a stony stare, silence, or if we were very graced, a brief nod of reply. In the end we just gave up and cycled silently onwards.

But we couldn't help asking ourselves why? From our accents I guess everyone we spoke to soon worked out we were British, even though our bikes were unadorned with either the Union Jack, or the Cross of St George. Could it have been because of the recent Brexit vote and the fact that we were seen as some kind of European deserters? Or do the Belgians treat everyone they don't personally know in the same way? I suspect the latter.

This was partly confirmed during our second day of travel on our way to Antwerp. On the outskirts of Sint-Niklaas, outside a row of immaculate, large detached houses, on a well-used cycle path, we came across an elderly lady entangled in an electric cycle, laying obviously injured at the bottom of a dry ditch. Despite several cyclists tootling by her, no-one had stopped to help, or even seem to recognise she was in need of help. We did stop, and as Fenella climbed down into the ditch to her, I ran and knocked on the door of the house to ask the owners to phone for an ambulance. It was at this point I realised my Yorkshire accented Dutch was nowhere as strong as I would have liked, I'd had very little practice of saying, 'excuse me for disturbing you, but there is an old lady wrapped around a bike, injured with a suspect broken collar bone, distressed and laying in a ditch at the top of your front garden.' So, not wanting to waste time with useless hand signals, as soon as the homeowner opened his front door I grabbed him by the arm and yanked him to the end of his driveway and pointed to where the old lady lay. What did I say about not knocking on any doors to disturb people? Anyway, my tactic worked and he soon scuttled back inside to phone for assistance. I went back to help Fenella and between us we disentangled the lady from her bike, and did our best to comfort and reassure her. Yet, still folk drove, walked and cycled passed us without stopping to help or even enquire about what was happening. For all they knew Fenella and I could have pushed the old dear into the ditch and was robbing her of her valuables! Even after the man of the house had made his telephone calls and reappeared, I'm sure it was only to make sure we weren't untidying his front lawn, and the only practical thing he contributed to the situation was to take the old ladies bike and inspect it for any damage. He never spoke to her once.

Nevertheless, his next door neighbour did eventually appear on the scene, but he seemed more interested in our bikes than the old lady, and as we waited for the ambulance to arrive, his conversation revolved around informing us that English bikes were definitely inferior to Belgian bikes, and that unlike their British equivalents, Belgium cities and towns were really beautiful places brimming with the splendours of architecture, art and culture.

Strange folk or what?

The difference between the Belgians and the Dutch was reinforced a couple of days later as we crossed the border into Holland. On the Dutch side sat a couple of cyclists, who as soon as we gratefully swapped Belgium for Holland, these two affable folk welcomed us and began a long friendly conversation about how they found Britain to be such a great place to visit, how we would enjoy Holland, and they even complimented us on our choice of British made bikes!

Nonetheless, I want to explore Belgium some more, deep down I consider I've read the Belgium's wrong. Reflection leads me to believe as a nation they are just cautiously reserved folk. A people who perhaps look towards our island with a sort of sad despair of what we have become, as we follow a 'USA based, speed driven, use-today-throwaway-tomorrow', way of life, rather than a slower, relaxed 'enjoy what you have', European way of living. We must go back.

16 April 2017

As summer approaches and I dither with my exact Velodyssee route, other choices have to be made. Perhaps the most crucial being, which bike to use? Thankfully, I have a bit of a choice. I'd narrowed my decision down to three bikes, but none were really suitable. Although, Rocky, my trusty Giant companion of LEJOG was worth considering. However, realistically he was a tad too small and he needed some desperate TLC. Since finishing at John o'Groats I'd never taken him out on the road again. In fact he'd been placed at the back of the garage, shrouded in dust sheets, and I suspect, much to my other bikes joys, seemingly abandoned and forgotten. Until this weekend that is. So, following a needy service, and a good clean and oiling, today Rocky once again hit the roads and cycle-ways of Yorkshire. Which got me thinking back to when Rocky and I last shared the roads of Yorkshire, as another rider rode his Giant bike......

When the second stage of the le Tour swept close by this area, within the peloton was the German rider and Stage 1 winner, Marcel Kittel. As I huffed and puffed up along the North Yorkshire lanes, I reasoned Marcel and me had a few things in common; we were both wearing yellow tops, admittedly mine was a reflective yellow safety bib provided free from Humberside Police, with

'Someone's Son' stamped across the front, (they couldn't find one with 'Someone's Dad' written on), whilst his was the Maillot Jaune of the Le Tour leader and was a specifically designed replica of the 1951 historic flat seamed collared Yellow Jersey from Le Coq Sportif, re-interpreted to include the famous white rose of Yorkshire. We were both riding Giant bikes, Marcel's being a Propel Advanced SL road bike, tailored to fit his body shape by Giant, with teardrop tubes, using electronic Giant Shimano gearing and brakes, with the front callipers incorporated within the fork blading, and every other component engineered to adopt a low profile to ensure an ultra-smooth aerodynamic air flow. Mine was Rocky, a self-adapted mountain bike bought in a closing down sale at Bridlington. Similarly, we were both at our peaks of fitness; Marcel had been through eight months of dedicated team training, overseen by the team's fitness coaches, doctors and dieticians who had placed him on a specially designed high protein/high carbohydrate regime, and I had cycled from home to the Humber Bridge a couple of times and stopped eating as much cheese.....

But to my disappointment I knew despite my liking for such a grand machine, Rocky wasn't the right bike for this trip. Oh dear was I about to break out into a cold sweat of worry... was I going to have to spend money?

24 April 2017

While at York on a short holiday my plan was to begin some real training for my Velodyssee trip. But on the second day some scumbag nicked my bike. Not Rocky, but Maud my much loved trusty 1980's folder; my caravan bike.

On the same day I was bitten by some creature or other. Being out of South Yorkshire and in the wilds further north, I naturally thought of 'snake'. But just how it had managed to get me on the ribcage I can't say. Reluctantly I had to agree with Fenella and accept it was probably a midge bite. However, shortly afterwards I began to suffer with a sore throat and headache, oh no, now I've got Malaria I reasoned. Next my symptoms caused me to run to the loo every hour or so, obviously I now had kidney failure. Soon my sore throat had me coughing and spluttering; acute bronchitis, glandular fever, double pneumonia? I could understand Fenella was deeply worried, so off she rushed in the car. Near to where we are staying is a private health clinic, York's equivalent to Harley Street. No doubt she's going to bring some highly qualified specialist to see me I reckoned. But on her return she said, 'I've been to Tesco, here's some Lemsips'. Could they possibly do the trick?

I wonder what's wrong with me.

Ps. For all of you who were deeply concerned, as I know many of you were but just didn't want to demonstrate your worries at the time, as I write this in September 2017 and the completion of my Velodyssee, I've still got the scar from when I was bitten………. Midge bite my…..

27th April 2017

First decent run of the season beginning tomorrow. Heading to Hyde, Manchester, on Friday, along the Trans Pennine Trail. Then following the River Mersey to Runcorn and then down to Chester on Saturday. This should see me cycling around 70 miles each day, crossing over the Pennine's on the first day, skirting Woodhead Pass and onto the flatlands of North Cheshire for day two. Looks like clement weather is on the cards, just hope the Lemsips work Ok.

8th May 2017

Following last weekend's high mileage training, this weekend has proved to be a big disappointment, with no miles completed. Unfortunately, illness has struck me down again. At first I thought it was my malaria flaring-up again, but I'm afraid it could be worse. Over the last week, more than once, I've fancied sardines on toast for lunch, in conjunction with this both me and Monet the cat have been experiencing sore eyes and sneezing of a morning. So yes, you've guessed it, the symptoms are all there; I've gone and gotten cat flu. Even Fenella is with me on this and has replaced my Lemsips with the 'hard stuff', now I'm on Beechams max strength cold and flu tablets. Oh woe is me, I hope I don't start with fur-balls!

10th May 2017

Well, what a period of non-cycling. My lacklustre energy levels have hit a new low. From Fenella putting me on a course of Beechams, after disagreeing with my self-diagnosis of cat flu, my doc has now got me on a course of penicillin! While Monet the cat seems to have fully recovered. The irony is that today was going to see my JustGiving page go live outlining final details of my proposed route. But it seems daft to upload it at the moment. But not to worry, hopefully like Monet, I'll soon be up and about, but instead of chasing rabbits, I hope to be chasing the miles down and looking to upload my route.

14th May 2017

Another disappointing week mile-wise as I still haven't been well enough to be able to get on my bike, still on the penicillin. However, my mood brightened considerably with the arrival of these beauties; technically gel padded undershorts, I prefer to think of them as bouncy-pants. Fantastic for the discerning cyclist who wants to swap their close fitting lycra shorts and instead wear cargo shorts, yet still have a degree of saddle protection. But, I can imagine greater possibilities. I believe they would be brilliant for everyone in most social occasions, both casual and formal. For there you can reside in padded comfort, confident in the knowledge that all under-parts are secure and sound. So, the next time you witness someone shuffle their nethers with a sly air of smugness, give them a wink and think to yourself, 'yes I know, it's all gel and no lotion'.

19ᵗʰ May 2017

So, starting to feel a little stronger and may be able to get out on the bike in a few days' time, I sorely need to get some miles under my belt. Nevertheless, it's time to tell of my proposed La Velodyssee route. My aim is to cycle in 3 countries, England, France and Spain. I plan to begin in Braunton north Devon and cycle to Plymouth via the NCR 27, the Devon Coast to Coast Route. Next, ferry to Roscoff and cycle down the west coast of France, heading through Nantes, St-Gilles-Croix-de-Vie, Les Sables-d'Olonne, Royan, Biarritz and Hendaye, the last town in France before the Spanish border. Then it's up, up and away into the Pyrenees, and on to San Sebastián in Northern Spain. Therefore, I begin in the north and finish in the north, I guess it's my bizarre version of the autumn racing classic, 'The Hell of the North'. The route via road is just over 1000 miles, but cycle-wise will probably be around 1200 miles as its 80% off-road, and I can never manage to cycle in a straight line for long.

I am cycling for Yorkshire Cancer Research and I have set-up an online JustGiving page which can be found at:

www.justgiving.com/fundraising/Mike-Banks4

I have also uploaded a sponsor poster which can be downloaded and used as you wish. Of course although

I'm doing the cycling bit, I'm only the lesser half of the team, the other being Fenella, my support driver, map reader, route finder and thousand-and-one organiser. Anyway, just to say many thanks for your interest and support, and fingers and other bits crossed, the show can now start to begin.

28th May 2017

It always seemed too big a call for Quintana to do the double, and in the end I think Tom Dumoulin was a worthy winner of the Giro d' Italia. So, I guess that leaves Froome and hopefully, Thomas, to completely spoil Nairo's dreams in Le Tour during July.

Unfortunately, I'm going to miss most of the live action between the trios, as I should be on my own 'velo' of despair during their Gaelic cycling tussles. Also, despite my best attempts, the similarity is likely to end at that junction too, as I won't even be able to claim to be riding on a road bike either. Following my lack of training over the last few weeks I thought yesterday afternoon was a good time to dust myself, and my old Raleigh Sprint, down and head out for a spin along the South Yorkshire lanes, as I thought my Sprint may be a good bike to take along as a spare during my Velodyssee. But, what an uncomfortable experience it turned out to be, for both the unfortunate folk who were unlucky enough to witness my pathetic attempts of sportif grandeur, and my poor aging body. Within 10 miles I had; head, shoulder, neck, back, wrist, elbow and foot pains. As for the bit (the large bit I should add) of me that encountered the saddle, it doesn't even bear (bare?) thinking about. I've just got to accept that I'm not the right shape for balancing on a lightweight road bike anymore, there's just too much bodily over-hang! But not to worry, I've decided to take the European approach to cycling, i.e. comfort over speed, as I think, aerodynamically, that could be my best bet for survival. In other words, I may invest in a laid-back French, Dutch (German??) bike as a spare, or maybe even as my main bike, a bike that won't seem so out of place as I greedily munch on olives and cheese and sip red wine during overly-long, leisurely lunch breaks. However, this may prove annoying for my team-mate Fenella, as of course, despite the European love of wine, she cannot even take a sip and drive. But, as far as I know 'tiddlyness' when cycling is not yet a criminal offence in France and Spain. Poor Fenella.

3rd June 2017

As the politicians headed to Yorkshire this week for an Election Question Time special, I managed a few miles on a selection of bikes including a new Royal Dutch Gazelle, from Cycle Heaven in York, which Fenella wanted me to purchase. But I wasn't tempted to risk opening my wallet and letting the 21st century in. But phew, what a close call! But as a change from cycling I took myself off for a hike around the Doncaster Way (17 miles). Just as I finished my ramble, I nearly ended-up under the wheels of a car. As I walked, rather painfully along the pavement, a driver pulled out of a supermarket car park and ran straight into me. Luckily she was only travelling very slowly, but nevertheless I still ended-up on her car bonnet. Now I've seen many a movie where the hero clings manfully onto a speeding '66 Chrysler Imperial, or a '75 Ford Gran Torin, under a New York underpass, or on Golden Gate Bridge, shouting threats at car-loads of snarling gangsters. But it just didn't seem to be like that for me whatsoever as I perched precariously on the front end of a Vauxhall Corsa in a Sainsbury's car park exit. To make me feel even more insubstantial the driver didn't even realise I was there until her daughter shouted 'Mam, there's an old bloke on the car bonnet with a beard'. At this point the driver suddenly stopped allowing me to slide ungracefully back to the terra-firma. To be honest I believe the only reason why she stopped so quickly wasn't for any concerns about my safety, rather I got the impression she was filled with dread in case Jeremy Corbyn had leapt on her car in a last minute bid for her vote. However in future I'm gonna vote for riding my bike, it's safer than walking the pavements of Doncaster!

16th June 2017

It's getting closer to blast off for my Velodyssee, I know this because my worry monitor is beginning to tickle the red zone! Still, I'm getting a few miles under my belt and I enjoyed a short, sharp blast in Lincolnshire with my good buddy Graham last Sunday morning, thanks Graham. Now I've got to the point where most of the organisation is nearing completion, all my mapping, and route details are completed, clothing and most equipment is sorted, including; a new tent and camping gear, an all-dancing-and-singing bike GPS unit, 2 pairs of fancy cycling sunglasses (well, 1 pair really, the other came from a sale at ASDA), a new helmet, shorts, T-shirts, cycling socks and a Volvo for Fenella. Nevertheless, I seem to be missing one item that I think I may need for my bike ride....a bike. I've got my old mountain bike, but having discovered on my LEJOG trip, it's a bit on the small side, in fact, as a bike for a long tour its way too small for me being only an 18" frame. But, I have been searching, I've even been to 3 very expensive cycle shops without getting thrown out when I mentioned how much I was willing to spend. Three figures for a bike still seems outrageous to me, especially, when the first figure becomes more than two! But, it seems I'm just gonna have to grin and bear it and despite my worst fears, I'll have to try and reach towards the bottom of my wallet for that very elusive currency. Whatever did happen to half-crowns?

But what about buying a car? It was time. Fenella's V70 was nearer in miles to 200K than 100K, but over the years it has been a bloody great car. One worry of its replacement is all the unfathomable technology it holds, including a voice operated satnav system. It'll be no good me trying to use it in France, my Yorkshire accented pronunciation of French is so bad it may just turn itself off in disgust. One example of this is a few years ago, being brave, I ordered 3 draft beers from a snooty looking waiter in Les Sables, which he diligently brought to the table, only to say, *'by, tha gev' that gud go mi owd mate, but tha nos', thee really ordered 3 boots o' beer instead'*. It turned out he was a student from Wakefield working a summer job in France, and as soon as I began my ineffectual muttering he knew I hailed from Yorkshire, so he had a silent giggle to himself and acted the pretentious waitron for a while. Hey ho. Beware France, as I said, it's getting towards time!

17th June 2017

Seem to have made it into the local paper this week!

For anyone bored enough to wonder what the article says, it says the following:

Stamina:

Doncaster Dad Gets ready for another major fund raising fete for cancer.

Three-country challenge bid.

A bit of bronchitis won't deter Thornensian Mike Banks from his second great fundraising challenge, cycling over 1000 miles through three countries, and largely on off-road terrain.

Mike, 62, will set off on July 2, on the Devon coast to coast route from Braunton to Plymouth, before crossing the Channel from Plymouth to Roscoff in France. He will tackle 'La Velodyssee' cycle route down the west coast of France and cross the Pyrenees into Spain to finish in San Sebastián.

Just recovering from bronchitis, Mike, who works as a Dyslexia Assessor, is raising cash for Yorkshire Cancer

Research. He lost both parents to the disease and has had skin cancer himself in recent years.

Mike said: "The distance and terrains will naturally prove to be challenges in themselves, but I believe the biggest test lies in folk having to unfortunately witness me being attired in fluorescent lycra for such a period of time!

"A few years ago I cycled from John O'Groats to Land's End as part of a triple challenge and then wrote a book about it. I will write another after this ride and half the proceeds from sales will go to YCR too."

Mike's Velodyssee Blog can be found at: **Mike's La Velodyssee Blog.** To sponsor him and help build up the coffers for Yorkshire Cancer Research visit:

www.justgiving.com/fundraising/Mike-Banks

24th June 2017

You know when you go into a shop seeking specialist advice, but you end up getting treated like a twit, well it happened to me today in Halfords at Scunthorpe. I wanted specific advice about a rather expensive bike I was thinking of buying, but I was spoken to as if I didn't know a handlebar from a seat post. I had no option other than to leave without even buying a spare inner tube, never mind the bike. I then went to the Cube Store in Scunthorpe and was treated exactly the opposite. There I met Tony who listened to my requirements and treated me like a cyclist who had a vague notion about what is and what isn't a decent bike. On top of this he provided me with expert knowledge without once being condescending or aloof. This is the type of folk all specialist shops should employ, and it pays off. For at last, with Tony's help and advice I've got my bike for my Velodyssee. It's a Cube Touring Pro 2017, aluminium, front suspension, disc braked, 24 gear, touring geometry framed beauty of a bike. It comes with Shimano M324 SPD clip pedals, full mudguards, chain guard, ergonomic grips, pannier rack and rear chainstay stand. It's being built over the weekend and will be ready to ride mid-week. A close call time-wise, but thanks Tony, you've made me a happy old man.

1 July 2017

We were due to leave for Devon this morning. But one thing I hadn't had chance to try-out was putting my new bike on my cycle carrier. Unfortunately when I did have a go this morning I couldn't get the bike to fit properly without scouring most of the paintwork from its frame! Therefore, it was a rush into Doncaster to buy a new towball mounted carrier. The only one we could get needed completely building up, including fitting of lights. With Fenella artfully and succinctly reading instructions and me ineffectually and frustratingly wielding multiple tools it was well gone lunchtime when we had finished. We tried again, but for ages couldn't figure out how to make the bike appropriately secure and it wasn't until 4.30pm that we managed to hit the road. So not the best start, and we didn't make North Devon until 10pm. Most places to eat were closed and all we could find were the left-over bits-and-bobs from Squires Fish Restaurant, not as dire as it sounds, just not a very balanced pre-start meal. Nevertheless, still on track to be Spain bound tomorrow morning and hopefully, should make Okehampton late afternoon.

2nd July 2017

First things first, please excuse any spelling mistakes or peculiar words, it's not all down to exhaustion, I've misplaced my specs and I'm writing this blog using Fenella's. I've no doubt they'll turn-up at some point. Made it to Okehampton at about 5pm, so first day more or less to plan. I only got lost once, however it was for about 2hrs! But, I take comfort in the fact that even Fenella couldn't figure out the correct route. The problem wasn't down to poor signage, it was more to do with the fact there were no route signs at all past Bideford. They just stopped full stop. Thank you Sustrans! In the end I had no choice other than to battle the Sunday drivers on a couple of A roads. But, on the positive side my bike ran excellently and it's beginning to feel like it's my bike now. Also stopped in a great B&B last night and found an old Manor House for tonight. Heading to Plymouth tomorrow and should make the ferry port around teatime.

3rd July 2017

A quiet bizarre day of cycling today; I didn't get lost once! Very strange. A lot of hills though, mostly of the up kind. Of the 41 miles covered 28 were uphill, followed by a glorious 13 mile descent into Plymouth. Arrived at 3.30pm so not such a long day in the saddle.

So, plenty of time to sup some Doombar Ale and get some snap before the 10pm ferry to Roscoff. Look out France, we're coming.

5th July 2017

Been out of connection for a couple of days, but this campsite has the magic of the interweb. Firstly the good news. Many thanks for all your charity donations, to date we've managed to raise one and a half times more than my original target. Brilliant. Also my bike, which I've began to call Pablo, as he liked his Cubes and after all, I am heading for Spain, is running like a dream and eating up the miles like a 'gud un, so a big thanks to Tony and all at Scunny Cube Store. Now for the usual 'me' occurrences of a cycle trip. Because I initially found it difficult to use my SDP pedals I decided some technical adjustment was required. Trouble was I think my technical adjustments were a touch on the vigorous side, as the bits I adjusted aren't there anymore, they've fallen off somewhere along the way – sorry Tony. The next bit of 'Michaelism' stems from me ensuring my Velodyssee Route Book is stored in a safe place. It is. It's stored in the bookcase in the lounge at home. I've forgotten to pack the bloody thing! But not to worry I'm still on track. Covered 60K from Roscoff to Scrignag yesterday and 70K to Gouarec today. Great cycling through woodlands and canal towpaths. Looking forward to a long night napping tonight. Starting to turn eastwards and beginning the run towards Nantes tomorrow.

6th July 2017

Some days of cycling are strange, mine seem to alternate between the weird and the peculiar. It began with frustration as at the first junction I faced a route diversion, which was so poorly signed I was off route until mid-afternoon. More by luck than judgement I managed to end-up in the correct town. But despite a frustrated search I just couldn't find the route out of the place. Although I did cycle one bike route for about 6 miles in a beautiful circle, only to end-up where I started. With temps in the mid 30's I met Fenella at about 4.30pm in Pontivy, where the only place we found open was the Hotel Du Chateau. While having coffee we decided to book in for the night. We then drove back to Gourec to de-camp. Back at the hotel we asked for a decent place to eat and was told of a restaurant just down the road. It was a nice little place. Just as we finished eating another British couple were paying their bill and Fenella remarked to the lady 'isn't it funny that we women end up at the till first'. From that we got chatting and it turned out they were Barry and Joan from Bolton, on the penultimate day of being filmed for A Place in the Sun, Home or Away. It also turns out the rest of the crew including the famed Jonnie Irwin are all kipping at our hotel. From our nattering's we have a good idea of whether Barry and Joan will buy, and if it's Home or Away. But to discover that answer for yourself watch sometime in September. They were also fascinated in our trip and promised to tell the rest of the crew about our plans. We should meet up for breakfast tomorrow. To keep the English connection alive arriving back at the hotel we turned on the TV only to see Wakefield and Castleford Rugby League 13's scrapping it out.

7th July 2017

Brilliant cycling today. Followed the Nantes/Brest canal from Pontivy to Le Roc, 70km. Fantastic surface all of the way and camping right alongside of the Velodyssee Route. Said goodbye to Jonnie and co, but I'll still not say if Barry and Joan will buy home or away. Fenella had a natter with a few of the crew after I'd left, although some had gone off filming another episode, as they film more than one at a time. They told her that they can spend 9 months on the road at a time, with occasional breaks at home. So not quite as easy and glamorous as it may seem when on TV and it must take its toll on the crew. This can be evidenced in the state and lateness our Jonnie stumbled down for breakfast. As he slurped strong black coffee and gingerly munched a couple of small dry bread rolls, Joan began telling him about our trip, my plan to ride down to Spain, but this only confused his muddled presenter's mind more and couldn't understand if I was stopping in a hotel in the middle of French town, just where I'd left my horse!

Nevertheless a good day's riding, albeit on two wheels. Also, I managed a first today; I ran over a snake! I actually thought it was a thin branch until I saw its little pointed tongue pop out just before my front wheel ran over it. It didn't yelp though, and when I went back for another look it had slithered away into the undergrowth. I don't know what breed of snake it was, so I am giving it the name 'Schwalbe Spicer Track Snake', after the indents left by my tyres and where it was sunning itself.

9th July 2017

Just a short catch-up as we hide in a hotel away from the thunder storms over Nantes tonight. Seven days cycling has taken us from Braunton in North Devon, to the outskirts of Nantes. Covered around 450 miles, and according to Google ascended 7782 feet and descended 7736 feet, it's been a bit up and down. The locals tell us it's been unusually hot, with temps in the mid to high 30's. But temps are forecast to drop during the next week. Met many touring cyclists but as yet none doing the Velodyssee. Should cross Nantes tomorrow and head towards the Loire estuary, and then south hugging the west coast. That makes us slightly ahead of my loose schedule, but haven't had a rest day yet. On average cycling around 6 hours a day and body holding up ok to date; although it is fair to say Fenella looks in much better nick than me, so no change there then. Pablo still running great, looking a bit dusty and will give his running gear a good spray of oil tomorrow morning.

10th July 2017

I knew crossing Nantes would be fraught, but to be honest crossing it, crossed me far more than I did it. Like most big cities it was easy to cycle your way in, but damn near impossible to find a straightforward cycle route out. I only covered about 35 miles route-wise, but I cycled for 7 hours, so you can guess how long I cycled in bloody frustrating circles looking for my route signs. In the end I made it to Le Pellerin at about 6.15pm. Even when I found my route it was an uncomfortable ride as I zig-zagged up and down the South Bank of the Loire for about 15 miles, without catching sight of the river until I arrived at Le Pellerin. When I did finally arrive I found the river to be a mucky brown slop of soup, the town having seen better days and the only interesting photo I could find was of a tree eating a car at the bottom of someone's garden. We then discovered that Le Pellerin is twinned with North Ferriby, says it all I guess!

Nevertheless, we found an interesting place to stay for the night in a little complex of Gites, seemingly run on the same principle as Southfork in the TV series Dallas. There was a mini Sue Ellen to greet us at the electronic gates and talkatively show us her estate, all the while mini Bobby stayed out of sight, presumably still in dreamland fretting about being shot and worrying about having to make a live appearance. After eating out in Pornic we bid goodnight to Sue and Bob and promptly fell asleep. I was awoken by a strange clomping. Turning on the light I found a grasshopper, who from the size and noise he was making, must have been directly related to Skippy the Bush Kangaroo. Opening the bathroom door there were so many strange night time creatures flying around it was like stepping into Jurassic Park. Fenella used so much insecticide spray she set the fire alarm going! It took us a good 15 minutes to clear the results of her assault up. In the end we just chucked them out of the window. I'm not sure if it was a Dodo I lobbed out, it just went out along with the peregrine, pelican and the penguin. I wonder what joys tomorrow will bring.

11th July 2017

Set off for Pornic to reach the west coast today. Initially I had trouble with flies. But after a while I changed back into my usual style of shorts. The problem with my first pair was they were a little too large around the waist, yet too small around the leg, therefore as I cycled along my pedalling action caused my shorts to slip down with the flies part ending-up near my crossbar. Oh what trials a cyclist must face. The good news is I bumped into the west coast at about 3pm. So, fingers crossed if I can manage to keep the big blue wet stuff on my right-hand side, navigation should be that bit simpler. Which is a bit of a relief, as I've realised today I've forgot to bring along the charging unit for my all-singing-all-dancing cycle GPS unit. No doubt it's safe and sound with my Velodyssee Route Book, at home in the lounge. Start down the west coast tomorrow.

13th July 2017

I don't know if you remember the TV series, and a crap film with someone out of Friends in it, called Lost in Space, well that's where I met Hans. Not Hans Solo, but Hans Ghertt, a German cycle tourist, who like me, was also lost in space; the space between two overlapping French maps. We were both having difficulty relating our maps to the roads we were cycling, they just didn't seem to match-up. My worry was we had to hit the causeway to Ile du Noirmoutier at low tide or we would end up stuck on the mainland until tide change, or get very wet trying to cross. Hans was unaware of this until after a confusing trek across the vastness of the space on our maps, we reached the causeway just in time to see the digital display read in three languages, one being German, **'FLOOD ALERT - GEFAHR DER DROWNING',** oh my God', proclaimed Hans, now I know what you mean! We met Fenella, who was waiting our arrival, and after assuring each other we could both swim, followed by a short, part English, part German and part panic discussion we decided to risk the crossing. So off the two of us went as fast as our aching legs would allow. But in reality there was no need to worry it turned out we had plenty of time to make it ok. This meant we made it on and off the Isle to finish at St Jean de Mont's at about 6.30pm. Here Hans and I bid farewell, he to find a campsite and me to meet Fenella. However, as Hans is on a three month cycle trip to Portugal, I really do hope we meet up again, is was brilliant to cycle with someone for a while and have a good natter putting the world to right from the perspective of a cycle saddle.

It's good to reach St Jean de Mont's because it means we've crossed the Velodyssee meridian, we're just over half way! A good time to take stock. Overall I think we're both in fairly good nick. We both have a good number of midge bites curtesy of Sue and Bobby at Southfork, but otherwise we're doing ok. As for me I put it down to my recent embracement of cycling technology and science. I still believe my Udderly Smooth chamois cream has magic properties or my bike saddle and bum would now be in serious dispute, but no problems in that particular region. While cycling I tend only to nibble fruit and nuts, along with the occasional electrolyte jelly (and I admit, an occasional beer) that seems to be more than adequate for me food wise. I then load up with protein and carbs on an evening. When I've finished cycling I also have 600ml of a recovery drink called Torq that Tony at Cube told me about. To be honest I hate the taste of it, but boy does it work. No overnight aches or pains. Also using proper cycling shoes instead of my usual converse shoes has made a tremendous difference. Although, I hated paying so much for them, in fact my shoes alone cost more than the cost of my last two bikes put together. Although, these bikes were bought on eBay. And of course there's the bike itself. A brilliant piece of engineering, it's as if some German engineer sat down and thought to themselves, 'right mi owd mucker, let mi get crackin' an design a bike fo daft owd sod up in Yorkshire who thinks he can do t'Velodyssee', and they did and I've gone and got it. So all in all, we dong good I thinks.

14th July 2017

I've been easy rider today. Cycled from St Jean de Mont's to Les Sables. A route I know well and one on my favourite cycle routes. Bypassing the campsites of St

Jean then throughout the wooded sand dunes between St Gilles and Les Sables, shady riding with a wonderful back breeze. Finished riding at about 3.30pm so not a long day in the saddle. Camping South of Les Sables and begin a two day ride to La Rochelle tomorrow. Just finished eating sausage, potatoes and French beans washed down with a bottle of local red. Strawberry tart to finish off with, just need to down my chocolate-mint Torq recovery drink, then my coach may allow a small bourbon and dark chocolate.

15th July 2017

Some mornings my first reading is supposed to be the 'Captain's Log', usually about someone's daughter's dancing class or a bloody Wookie convention somewhere. But some mornings my reading must be my cycling map of mid-west France. I plan to keep practising with the latter until I achieve accuracy. Although Fenella is positive if I wore my specs so I could see what I'm reading and could also see the route signs, meaning I'd need much less practice. Still I made it to 30K from La Rochelle today, despite a disturbed night as the locals went to town celebrating Bastille night. Passed a few vineyards and mussel beds on-route today.

Camping at L'Agiinols and just watched the end of today's stage of Le tour while drinking Grimsberg Cherry beer.

16th July 2017

It's been a day of discovery for me. Apparently not all places in France are wonderful, some are quite frankly a bit of a dive. I've also learnt that while fields of sunflowers look great on TV as Le tour sweeps past, when you actually cycle up close, sometimes on a track through the middle of a field full of 'em, they are literally buzzing with life. Most of it the flying and stinging kind. Luckily I didn't get stung but I've had flies and other creepy-crawlies in my ears, nose, eyes and one spider tried for my mouth.

It's also been hard, hot cycling in 35°c+ heat all day. Made it to La Rochelle about 5pm but found a large music festival in full swing, meaning neither myself nor Fenella could find where each other was. Finally found each other at 6.30pm. The temp in Fenella's car read 42°c! Found a very nice hotel who recommended a great fish restaurant where we sat next to a guy dressed in Valentino denim. That's the other thing I've learned today, apparently it is possible to buy jeans for more than £10 in places other than Matalan! Going to be even hotter tomorrow and I begin my longest section heading for Royan.

17th July 2017

I wonder if you can eat swan-burgers in France, after all there is no Queenie to complain? I've been across miles and miles of wetlands, mussel beds and frog's legs beds and seen plenty of herons, geese and ducks, but very few swans. It's been the hottest day today, so I had to adopt a different technique of cycling, and as Fenella is a much better cyclist then me, I chose to base my style on her mode of cycling; no rush, use an easy even cadence and let the miles take care of themselves. Rather than my rush and drop method of progress. It worked a treat, covered 80K and reached Marennes at about 5.50pm. First sections ran along a gorgeous coastline of sandy beaches and coves. Then headed inland to cross Rochford, not the place the cheese comes from, that has "q' in it, not a queue for the cheese, but a 'q' for the spelling. On the whole a good day signage wise, although the town elders of Rochford must be extremely pleased with a new gigantic road bridge built on the edge of town as all signage leads to the damn thing. In the end, because of a lack of route signs I had no option other than to cross the bloody thing. I then found myself on a dual carriageway, not the safest place I thinks. But no one ran me over, or even sounded their horns, I guess they maybe thought 'ah the Brits are abroad'. Weather forecast for tomorrow is still hot, but with a 100% chance of rain. Hopefully should reach Royan sometime in the afternoon.

18th July 2017

As I write we're in Royan on our hotel balcony watching the lightening out in the ocean, awaiting the predicted storm to arrive. We actually got to Royan at about 2pm, crossed the Gironne by ferry and made Soulac sur mer at 3.30pm, but couldn't find a hotel or campsite with room for us. We had to ferry back to Royan. But not to worry, looking at what's heading our way tonight's not the night to be in a tent. The coming storm must be the 100% rain that the BBC weather app told of, otherwise it's been another scorcher of a day. This part of France has a different 'air' about itself, I guess I must be getting close towards what is loosely called 'The South', but in my mind that's not until we hit Biarritz, my next major port of call. With the coming rain, hopefully with fingers crossed, the temps should fall tomorrow.

19th July 2017

Well it has been cooler today, mid 20's instead of mid 30's. So that was a bonus. But it's been a strange day of cycling. 90% of the day has been spent on deserted roads running through woodlands with only Cicadas for company. However, I did pass a naturist campsite. It's the only site I've seen with a barbed wire fence around it. I'm not sure if it's to keep the non-naturists out, or the naturists in, either way clambering over that fence would be an uncomfortable experience for either party, particularly those with dangly bits. Made it to Carcans Ocean at 5.30pm and my manager, coach, navigator, boss tells me I've just less than 200 miles left....given all the planning and hours on the saddle a strange (scary?) feeling indeed.

20th July 2017

Well in many ways it's been an interesting day. It didn't start too good, as over breakfast Navigator Fenella realised I'd worked my miles for the day completely wrong. Some were under calculated, some over calculated. Not a bad average to my way of thinking. But Fenella just sighed in exasperation and told me to go and find something I could manage without mishap. So I went to the loo. Only trouble was I chose the disabled/shared loo and initially I couldn't find the light switch for love-nor-money. I found it in the end though. As I peacefully went about my morning routine, I was disturbed from concentrations by a loud banging on the loo door and frantic shouting in French, seems I pressed the disabled assistance alarm several times while trying to turn the light on. I admit most times in life I do need assistance, but with this job I thought I was doing ok. More worrying was in all the confusion I'd forgotten I'd put my sunglasses in my hat, that was until I put my hat on my head, to find my specs had fallen into the loo.

Nevertheless, once on the bike I thought things would settle down. Not so, they started to settle up instead. In other words even before my legs had properly warmed up and my Sun specs dried I found myself climbing tree lined cliffs. In no time every muscle in my body was in anguish, and to have both muscles hurting at the same time was agony. This went on for 10 miles, rather than the 1.5 miles I'd originally calculated. However it did end eventually and I then had about 30 miles of undulating concrete roads, originally built in WW2 by German engineers to allow motorbike riders to travel north/south. But at least the French have now put them to a more peaceful usage.

Made it to Cap Ferret at 4pm, but I wouldn't board the ferry as they were just slinging bikes willy-nilly on to the back of the boat and I reckoned as Pablo has been so good to me so far on my Velodyssee I wasn't going to let some heavy handed deckhand treat him so crudely. So a bit of a wasted journey down the peninsula. But I guess as it's been commentated, it was always going to end outlandishly when you put someone from Yorkshire, a cap and a ferret all together in one location.

21st July 2017

A day from the ridiculous to the sublime, is all I can say. It began with using Pablo as part clothes-horse, part dustbin and part re-cycling unit followed by a cold shower, only a nectarine for breakfast and the facing of a long day in the saddle. It ended in a colour-themed spa hotel, a bathroom bigger than our tent, a beautiful three course dinner and......no cycling tomorrow; all at the organisation of Fenella. Cycling-wise I was back in the woods again, climbing, aching and fighting for oxygen. Here's a thing I don't entirely twig; how come I set-off cycling at sea level, climbed for 3 miles up dreadfully acute hills and then descend for all of 3 feet and ended up at a beach back at sea level? What is with hills when cycling, how is it they only seem to have an upside?

Well actually it was a beach at the side of a huge lake. So large I first thought I'd reached the ocean. I could just glimpse the far shore, oh my God I thought I've been so long in the saddle I can see North America, then rationale hit me and I thought, no, it can't be as I can't make out the politically sane out protesting. Otherwise not a pretty day scenic-wise as I followed a series of D roads to get about 85km done and dusted and a good way down to Biarritz.

Day off tomorrow reading and watching Le tour on TV, yippee!

23rd July 2017

I've noticed a couple of things today, firstly my helmet and cycling caps needed adjustment, making smaller, whist at the same time, without any saddle adjustment, I seem to be sat higher on my bike. My head is shrinking and my bum is getting more corpulent; I think I may be turning Dutch. No rain as yet, now predicted to arrive in the night, so a pleasant day on the bike. Covered about 90km, still mainly in undulating woodlands and finished cycling at 5pm at Vieux-Boucau-les-Bains. This hopefully should set me up nicely to cross Bayonne and get to Biarritz sometime tomorrow afternoon. We are based in Bayonne for the next couple of nights so should be able to meet Fenella at the hotel for lunch as I pass through. It's an Okko hotel and is very different to any we have used so far. Very Japanese themed. Nevertheless I was extremely pleased to discover, as we used the lift, finding the Archers playing away for our entertainment. I was even more surprised to hear Radio 4 playing on speakers outside the hotel. It wasn't until Fenella told me, 'it's not the hotel, it's you, you've got Radio 4, playing on your phone via the internet, duh'. Still, it was nice to catch up with the goings on in Ambridge a little. May get wet tomorrow.

24th July 2017

My goal for today was to reach Biarritz, but with permission from my trainer/manager I actually rode a little further. Having an early start I made my friend Amanda's old stamping ground, Bayonne by lunchtime. As I passed through I was surprised at just how many folk shouted for me to send their regards to Amanda, all except one cafe owner who chased me down the road demanding I settle one of her bills for 5 tart de citrons and 11 beers.

Following a strangely balanced lunch of popcorn, yoghurt, fruit and a couple of double expressos I set off and battled my way through Biarritz for 2.30pm By this time squally showers and the foothills of the Pyrenees had made their presence felt on both my comfort and my stamina. Eventually called it a day at Saint-Jean-de-Lux.

It proved to be another day with frustrating route signage, with cycle lanes suddenly finishing at junctions or roundabouts with no directions whatsoever of which way to go. The problem, one which has frustrated many cycle tourists using the Velodyssee maps, is their lack of detail other than the Velodyssee Route itself. Traffic free areas appear on the maps as a green blob, with towns and villages being depicted as just a large or small yellow coloured blob. Other nearby roads, rivers and canals are depicted as faint lines, all in the same washed-out blue hue, meaning if you happen to wander off the direct route you have no idea of exactly where you are, or which way to go. Nevertheless, the miles are ticking by nicely and the end of my journey is fast approaching.

25th July 2017

I've just dropped a peanut down my cycling shirt, but not to worry I'll eat it later. The reason for the peanuts is they go with the beer we're having in our hotel in Sans Sebastián. Yes! Made it to Spain, ha ha. Couldn't quite cycle entirely into the centre of Sans Sebastián as I didn't want to get arrested for cycling along the motorway I found myself on, so prudence ruled and I met Fenella at the first slip-road I came across. Still, as motorways go it was a very nice motorway and the Spanish drivers seemed more amused than annoyed with me. So, this is really just a short blog to say we did it! I'd originally planned to complete the journey in 24 cycling days, but managed to complete in 21 cycling days, so feeling a bit chuffed with myself.

25th July 2017

So it's done and dusted! I want to use this blog to say thanks to all who have supported me during my Velodyssee journey. Firstly, Fenella. There is absolutely no way I could have completed this trip without her selfless, fantastic and always willing love and support. Thanks Fenella. James has not had many mentions, but as I was absorbed in planning details and buying bikes

268

etc. James was in the process of buying his first house, not once did he ask me to drop things to help him, again selfless. Tony and the team at Scunthorpe Cube Store who gave me brilliant advice and helped me select my bike, who I've began to call Pablo. What a fantastic machine; England to Spain, mostly off road, estimated at about 1200-1400 miles without a single mechanical or even a puncture. So, thanks to you Pablo, 'thas one bloody good bike'. And then there is all you guys out there who have supported me all the way through my planning to completion. It's through your kind charity donations, wonderful comments and best wishes that I have been able to make it. As for me and what's next.....has any one got a detailed maps of.......?

Appendix II

Translations

Oops, het spijt me, excuse moi.' - 'Oops I'm sorry, excuse me.'

Je suis désolé monsieur, il est toujours comme ça quand il monte à vélo'
'I'm very sorry sir, my husband can be very silly when he's riding a bicycle.'
Flood Alert – Gefahr Der Drowning – Flood Alert – Danger of Drowning.

Bis später auf der Straße. – See you later along the road.

Vous pensez peut-être que je suis démodé avec votre lycra brillant et vos entraîneurs de fantaisie, vous pourriez penser que je suis passé devant, mais je vais vous montrer ce qu'un vieux soldat peut faire"! - 'You maybe think I'm outmoded with your bright lycra and your fancy trainers, you might think I'm past it, but I'll show you just what an old soldier can do'!

Pourquoi diable suis-je ici en train de faire ça? Mon Dieu! Que se passe-t-il si le vieil imbécile le déchire ici? L'embarras de cela; Que vais-je dire à Ascelina et Madieu pendant le déjeuner? - 'why the hell am I here doing this? Mon Dieu! What if the old fool croaks it out here, what will I do? The embarrassment of it; what will I tell Ascelina and Madieu over luncheon?

S'il vous plaît, pour l'amour de Dieu, emmenez un des enfants jusqu'à ce que nous arrivions au sommet, ou du moins, achetons le chien"! - Please, for God's sake, take one of the kids until we get to the top, or at least, buy the dog'!

Les arbres ne sont pas connus par leurs feuilles, ni même par leurs fleurs, mais par leurs fruits.' – 'The trees are not known by their leaves, or even by their flowers, but by their fruits.'

Ne vous inquiétez pas pour ces twerps arrogants, allez-y moi vieux, vouns y arriverez'. –
'Do not worry about these arrogant twerps, go ahead me old, you'll get there'.

Réveille-toi, Philippe, nous devons partir.' – 'Wake up Philip we have to leave.'

'Pour la femme pitoyée, fermez la bouche' – 'For pity's sake woman, shut your mouth.'

Appendix III

Further Reading

La Vélodyssée – L'aAtlantique à velo de Roscoff à Hendaye – Le Routard, Hachette Livre (Hatchett Tourisme) 2016.

https://www.bbc.co.uk/history/historic_figures/richard_i_king.shtml

https://www.bellefrance.com/holidays/charente/maritime-history/

https://www.brittany-cottage.me.uk/josselin.html

https://www.brittanytourism.com

https://www.brittanytourism.com/Destination Brocéliande › Josselin

https://www.brittanytourism.com/to-see-to-do/iconic-routes

https://www.ee.france.fr/en/discover/pornic

https://www.en.nates.fr/home.html

https://www.feel-planet.com/dune-of-pilat-france/

https://www.forum.axishistory.com/viewtopic.php?t=14
6941

https://www.france-atlantic.com/francofolies-french-music-festival-la-rochelle

https://www.france-voyage.com/tourism/sables-olonne-963.htm

https://www.french-waterways.com/waterways/west/nantes-brest/

https://www.independent.co.uk/travel/europe/a-tale-of-two-cities-biarritz-and-bayonne-1925686.html

https://www.lonelyplanet.com/france/southwestern-france/bayonne

https://www.lonelyplanet.com/france/southwestern-france/biarritz

https://www.lonelyplanet.com/france/southwestern-france/la-rochelle

https://www.planetepassion.eu/snakes-in-france/western-whip-snake-france.html

https://www.reserves-naturelles.org/dunes-et-marais-d-hourtin

https://www.revolvy.com/main/index.php?=Noirmoutie
r

https://www.talmondais.com/payre.html

https://www.telegraph.co.uk/news/0/bastille-day

https://www.the-french-atlantic-coast.com/2016/04/27/chatelaillon-plage-a-family-friendly-beach-resort-in-the-charente-maritime/

https://www.thespruce.com/jade-meaning-ancient-strength-and-serenity-1274373

https://www.tripadvisor.co.uk/Attraction_Review-g1079341-d10340692-Reviews-Lac_d_Hourtin_

https:www.//uk.france.fr/en/provence/article/cicadas

https://www.vendee-guide.co.uk/marais-poitevin.htm

https://www.vendee-guide.co.uk/vendee-history.htm

Printed in Great Britain
by Amazon